EX LIBRIS

....

Nemo's
ALMANAC

A Quiz for
Book Lovers

Edited by Ian Patterson

P

PROFILE BOOKS

First published in Great Britain in 2017 by
Profile Books Ltd
3 Holford Yard
Bevin Way
London WC1X 9HD
www.profilebooks.com

10 9 8 7 6 5 4 3 2 1

Selection and introduction copyright © Ian Patterson 2017
'Nemo's first century' copyright © Alan Hollinghurst

A CIP catalogue record for this book is available from the British Library.

ISBN: 978 1 78125 950 4
eISBN 978 1 78283 403 8

Text design and layout by sue@lambledesign.demon.co.uk

Printed and bound in Great Britain by Clays, Bungay, Suffolk

CONTENTS

INTRODUCTION

I first encountered the literary quiz called *Nemo's Almanac*
round about 1990, when Alan Hollinghurst was the editor.
A friend read an article about it and sent it to me, and I
was immediately captivated by the small, slightly austere
pamphlet with its thematically organised and, I thought,
completely mysterious quotations. For months I tried to track
them down, discovering new reference books in the library,
keeping my increasingly dog-eared *Nemo* in my pocket all the
time, phrases sometimes running round and round in my
head like earworms. I still didn't do very well: my first score
was 142 out of a possible 730. But I was hooked.

And I am not the only one to have fallen for its charm.
Nemo's Almanac has been quietly appearing every year since
1892. The first issues were called *Nemo's Illustrated Almanac*
and had a brief and apt quotation as a legend running along
the top of the front cover. (In 1895 it was 'Wit's Pedlar', the
following year 'This fellow picks up wit as pigeons peas'.)
In recent years it has settled down to a regular pattern of
quotations arranged according to monthly themes, but when
it started it was much more varied. For a start, it was an actual
almanac, including memorable anniversaries, phases of the
moon, saints' days and the like. A Twickenham widow and
governess called Annie E. Larden started selling it to a range
of subscribers in 1892 as a quiz that had 'evolved ... from a
holiday task set for her charges'.

More than a century has passed since then, and although it
has changed considerably over the years, the Almanac is still

going strong; in 1997 Alan Hollinghurst passed the editorship on to the late Gerard Benson, poet and anthologist (and one of the Barrow Poets, for readers with long memories); he was followed ten years later by the poet, actor and broadcaster Nigel Forde, who in 2016 handed the editorship to me. I hope that this book will attract many more competitors to the annual. The cultural world the competition finds itself in today is very far removed from its innocent earlier years. The internet has made it possible to track down even the most recondite of quotations in almost no time at all, which means that it ought to be possible to polish off a whole *Nemo* in an afternoon.

But why would anybody want to do that? If you deny yourself the instant gratification of Google and the vast array of available databases, you find that a whole hinterland of investigative possibility opens up. Finding quotations without electronic assistance means reading (or re-reading) novels, flipping through volumes of poetry and prose, poring over anthologies of writing from the last five centuries, day after day, month after month, for the best part of a year; looking for some half-remembered turn of phrase or description or snatch of dialogue, all for the unparalleled pleasure of the moment of discovery. And there are plenty of other pleasures, even sociable ones, to be found on the way ('Hey, listen, I didn't know X had written poems like this, did you?' and 'You remember when I said Y was such a turgid writer, and you disagreed? Well I've just been re-reading him, and I was right.') You can ask the advice of everyone you know, friends and relations, workmates, casual acquaintances. Some of the quotations, if I'm anything to go by, stick in your mind forever. Lines from Hugh MacDiarmid's poem, 'On a Raised Beach', for instance: 'I study you glout and gloss, but have / No cadrans to adjust you with' ran round my brain for so long that I'll never forget them. And for no particular reason, Edith Sitwell's words 'Said the musty Justice Mompesson' stuck too, probably because of the half-rhyme between 'musty' and 'Justice'. It's a matter of time. Like slow food, or long-distance walking, undertaking this might seem a luxury, a self-indulgence, or a waste of time, but like them it can be – and I would argue it is – beneficial and restorative. Competitors who subscribe to the pamphlet Almanac always have the best part of a year to work out their answers and send them in, so there's space for obsession to take hold, and plenty of time for leisurely investigations. The quotations in *Nemo's Almanac* often contain passing clues to the author's identity – some stylistic signature, some internal allusion or reference, or just the subject matter; but it can take a long time musing on them before they swim into focus. Writers are all different, just as people are different, and it's only by absorbing their work slowly that the range of their world view emerges.

In recent years, something of this pleasure has been lost. Our grandparents and their grandparents were used to storing things in their memories – information, stories, scraps of verse or whole poems, songs, hymns, chunks of the Bible. All this is differently available to us in our reliance on our electronic resources. The advantage we have is that most questions can be answered almost immediately. The disadvantage is that the knowledge (or information) we get that way seems to have less purchase on our minds and can disappear as quickly as it comes. In many ways, *Nemo's Almanac* might seem a strange and quaint survival, despite the extent to which it has changed since the 1890s, but though at first acquaintance it might appear out of place in the twenty-first century, in fact it is more engaging than ever. Both the process of searching and the writings themselves can strengthen parts of the mind the internet cannot reach. The rhythms of poetry, the balance and structure of well-written prose, the patterning of life into language – these can all take a stronger hold in our minds than the endless flow of information that now defines our lives. It also broadens our knowledge; speaking just for myself, I know that taking part in the competition over the last twenty-five years has led me to read hundreds of writers, and quantities of novels and poems I might never have thought of reading otherwise, from the poetry of Jan Struther, Charles Cotton and T. E. Brown to novels by Thackeray, William Plomer and May Sinclair, and I'm sure that the experience has widened my appreciation and deepened my understanding. And of course I've read many more novels, plays, and poems that *didn't* contain the quotation I was looking for than those that did – and that's good, too.

A hundred years ago, before they were abandoned, the direct questions in *Nemo* reflected a very different world. I don't know, for example, how I would set about answering a question like this one from 1902: 'By what three virtues is the frame of British freedom to be sustained?' (please don't send in your suggestions). Others were more allusive than this, such as 'How did Aunt Deborah know that the Squire was a bachelor?': hard to answer if you haven't read *Kate Coventry* by Whyte Melville, which these days practically nobody (including me) has. They sound halfway between crossword clues and the kind of questions favoured by Radio 4's 'Round Britain Quiz', or the Christmas quiz that appears in the *Guardian* each year set for the pupils of King William's College in the Isle of Man. *Nemo's* quotations, because they are just quotations, have none of this cryptic impenetrability. They are just quite hard to pin down. Not all of them – some are quite straightforwardly recognisable. But most take a bit of puzzling over and a bit of research.

The tone and the competitors have changed, too. In the early Almanacs, there was a note to reassure readers that 'Biblical allusions are never intended or allowed.' And as Alan Hollinghurst points out in his history of the quiz, there were some encouraging patriotic themes in the wartime editions. There are plenty of notable names among past competitors, too: bishops and aristocrats, civil servants, writers and academics (the literary critic Dame Helen Gardner was apparently famous for talking about nothing else at dinner parties and Oxford high tables, and made her research students look for answers, but to her great chagrin never actually achieved full marks, despite being a frequent runner-up). But while new names are added each year, the pseudonyms that many competitors once used have fallen out of fashion. Gone are 'The Mollpolls' and 'Merrytwang', 'Yam', 'Hilarius', and 'Badger', although one or two, like 'Gli Amici', still survive. As you enter into the quiz, and join the historic ranks of Nemo competitors, perhaps you will be tempted to resurrect this tradition and come up with your own. I still haven't settled on one myself, after nearly thirty years; but as editor, my pleasure has to come from choosing the quotations rather than tracking them down.

NEMO'S FIRST CENTURY

Alan Hollinghurst

For the first five years of its existence *Nemo's Almanac* was
an almanac in more than name: the pages of questions
faced wood-cuts of well-loved scenes (University College,
Aberystwyth, Bridlington Harbour, The Old Sulphur Well,
Harrogate) and a full calendar of anniversaries: Sydney lit
by gas (25 May 1841), earthquake at Menton (24 February
1887), Oldham Theatre burnt (6 April 1878), suicide of
Admiral Fitzroy (30 April 1875), the Clerkenwell explosion
(13 December 1867), birth of the Duchess of Albany (17
February 1861) – a catalogue of forgotten triumphs and
calamities. If the early issues were rather improving in tone,
that must be put down to the profession of the first Nemo,
Annie E. Larden, a Twickenham governess who evolved the
publication from a holiday task set for her charges, who gave
marks for 'neatness' and 'intelligence', and who observed
drily in her first annual notes that 'Competitors are advised
to persevere'. For all this the first edition was 'wonderfully
successful' (it made a profit of £5) and its formula was clearly
one that touched on a British passion for national literature
and history and a fondness for amateur sleuthing.

Literary quotations were interspersed with quite wide-
ranging questions – neither easy. One speciality was the
characterless one-liner ('The leaves fell russet golden and
blood-red', 'The sweetest song ear ever heard'); another
the query either tediously particular ('How many persons
connected with the Royal Family have been in the Navy since
the Accession of Henry VIII?') or impossible to ascertain

('What was the favourite colour of the ancient Irish?' – saffron, apparently). Clearly competitors thrived on these; in 1894 the question 'Did Oliver Cromwell use blotting paper?' drew a deeply researched answer from 'a competitor at the Cape'. Mrs Larden's farewell number asked recklessly for contestants to 'Mention some remarkable events in history of which you have been personally aware' – and in 'Old Nemo's last words' the following year (her retirement was as protracted as that of some great diva) she took the self-made opportunity to reminisce. She was 70 at the time and recalled gaining her 'first idea of public events from a Black Frock, worn with much pride, as mourning for William IV'. A touch miffed, one feels, that two competitors could remember the death of the Duke of York in 1827, she lets us know that Grimaldi's song, quoted in the Almanac for 1898, had been heard by her grandfather in London in 1814.

If such details open up a haunting perspective beyond the Almanac's own century, much else remains obscure. Who were the numerous competitors of these early years? Their names sound as indefinably fictional as their pseudonyms are whimsical. Pseudonyms were very much the norm, yielding up their secret only when their wearer won a prize. One longs to know more about 'Gypsy' and 'Mopsa', 'Two Bees' and 'Three Spiders', 'Lovey and Dovey', 'Tomatoes', 'Twee' and 'Mieux Sera'. 'Skids' was Mrs Pledge of Epsom; 'Botanist' the Countess of Mexborough. And who were Mrs Dobbo of Castle Dobbo, Co Antrim, Miss Clive Bayley of 'The Wilderness', Ascot, Miss Ina Clogstone and Lady Blanc of the rue de la Pompe, Paris? Titled ladies abounded in the marks list, and Mrs Larden (who had dedicated early editions of the Almanac to the Duchess of Sutherland and the Duchess of Leeds) was not above preening herself on her correspondents: under the heading of 'Claims to Distinction' she pointed out that Horatia Cocles, an entrant in 1901, was 'connected with Tower Bridge'.

When Ethel Marion Atkinson takes over as editor in 1902 at the age of 25 we find a distinct change in the Almanac's character: questions are phased out until by 1911 they have virtually disappeared; and thematic setting appears for the first time ('Great Men', 'Fair Cities', 'A Family Group') and will continue through the half-century of Miss Atkinson's reign, adapting only during the two world wars to reflect events beyond the backward-looking bookishness of the competition – 'Service', 'Struggle', 'Leaders' in 1916; 'Fortitude', 'Justice', even 'Resurrection' in 1942.

The picture we piece together of her own life is an endearing one: she had been introduced to Nemo as a teenager by Miss Champion, for a while the editor of Nemo's slightly younger sister Hide & Seek; an ardent Wagnerite as a young woman, she alters the entry date to accommodate her August visits to Bayreuth (the 1905 cover quotation is from Die Meistersinger); her home in Hersham, Surrey, is 'broken up' in 1933, when she asks competitors to tell her of 'a nice little house by the sea'; and the next year sees her in St David's, where she remains until her death in 1967 at the age of 90. In 1943 she is extending her sympathy to those who have lost their books in the blitz, and the following year she expresses (if in rather different terms) the problem which is Nemo's to this day: 'Between having no maid, nor daily help, – the garden, which must be done – savings group secretarial work, WI, and various other activities, it has really been difficult to find time. And house-work was the last straw!' It was during this time that the poet Katherine Watson, who seventeen years later was to become Nemo herself, was stationed at St David's and given the run of her library.

Perhaps Miss Atkinson was editor for too long. Though she lacked Mrs Larden's homiletic zeal, she was unshakeably conservative in taste, and over her half-century there is only a slight shift in the booklist on which she draws. Typical authors quoted are Owen Meredith, Bret Harte, Elizabeth

Barrett Browning, Whittier in 1909; Whyte Melville, Aytoun, Mrs Ewing in 1919 (though there are soon complaints that 'Nemo's choice of books is too modern'). In 1922, the great modernist year, the twentieth-century authors included arc Binyon, Masefield and Tagore; and over the coming decades Humbert Wolfe was to be her sole concession to the new. Miss Atkinson remained in essence a Victorian, promoting the reading of her own childhood ('Macaulay's letters are not yet out of date') even as she realised that the world was changing around her. In her last years she seems like a figure out of Miss Mitford, making jam and bottling fruit, sending news of a snowdrift ('the lifeboat fetched provisions') and regretting that 'the splendid education of the young gives them no time for the leisurely "Culture" in which most of us were brought up'. Meanwhile her circulation had plummeted and in 1945 she had only 19 competitors.

Her successor, in 1949, was Lady Birkett, née Dorothy Forbes, the wife of Sir Thomas Birkett, who had been Sheriff of Bombay during the Great War and subsequently retired to fish and shoot on an estate at Beldorney, Aberdeenshire. They were divorced in 1923, and the following year Lady Birkett was the first Nemo to produce a book of her own, the anthology *Hunting Ways and Hunting Lays*. After that she is hard to trace, and in the late 40s and 50s is found moving between a number of addresses in Belgravia and Bayswater: a cottage, a mews house, a flat above a milliner's shop. The current Lord Birkett (no relation) recalls that his mother received a letter from her, 'suggesting that she was the senior Lady Birkett, and why didn't my mother call herself by some other title'.

Lady Birkett's reign is marked by various attempts at improving the Almanac. The prizes are doubled (to £5, £2 and 10/-); she introduces new authors (T. S. Eliot, Lytton Strachey, Carl Sandburg, Auden, MacNeice, Christopher Fry), invites competitors to name their books of the year (*Kon-Tiki* and *The Boy with a Cart* in 1950), their favourite authors (significantly still Tennyson, Browning and Kipling; Dickens, Trollope and Lamb), and their Desert Island Books, 'as in the radio programme'. For all this, the Almanac's fortunes continued to decline, and by 1958 only 12 competitors were left.

Nonetheless, Lady Birkett was an excellent setter, who brought a new range and wit to the game; all her pages were thematic, and often on subjects, such as 'Cherry Stones' or 'Indigestion', that are not easy to find six or seven instances of. Eye trouble compelled her to give up (at I guess the age of about 70), and when Miss Watson took over in 1959 she maintained the freshness, breadth and virtuosity of her predecessor; and benefited too from some publicity – the first that the eccentric byway of the Almanac seems ever to have attracted. In 1960 a competitor had written about *Nemo* in the magazine *Books*; this lead to an article by Leonard Russell in the *Sunday Times*, which in turn stimulated a letter from Graham Greene, who had participated in a family Nemo syndicate as a boy. Circulation rose and many competitors still at work joined the list. Even so, it was only a cash injection from the US in 1966 that saved the Almanac from closure.

The demands of Miss Watson's Burford bookshop obliged her to give up in 1970, and John Fuller's accession was marked, as one might have expected from an Oxford don who is also a distinguished poet, by an increase in arcana (Coleridge notebook jottings known only to specialists, never reprinted anagrams by Joshua Sylvester) as well as in modernity (whether Empson or Highsmith, Redgrove or Angus Wilson). Publishing from his own Sycamore Press, and offering discounts for larger orders, Mr Fuller raised the circulation from 150 to 500 in three years, and a mention in the TLS in 1976 was to add several hundred more, many from the US. (Further publicity under the current editorship has brought the figure to 2,000* – big enough, perhaps, if the Almanac's

---

* This refers to Alan Hollinghurst's editorship, from 1988 to 1996.

air of innocent obscurity and cliquish obsessiveness is to be preserved.)

The social history of *Nemo's Almanac* would make a touching and revealing study. It would have to do with time and memory, class and literacy, friendship and rivalry, education and ethics. (The whole question of swopping, and indeed of cheating, over which earlier Nemos sought vainly to exercise control with bannings, penalties and separate lists for 'non-exchanging' competitors, would have to be looked into as well.) Longevity has characterised its addicts, Miss Champion (comp 1894–1930) and Miss Overton (who competed for 54 years and never won a prize) among them. The Hon Mrs Bontine ('one of the earliest Nemoites') was looking for quotations to within a fortnight of her death in 1928 at the age of 97 (though in her zeal she is outdone by Sir Charles Clay, alleged to have died with the words 'I've just found October 2' on his lips). 'Three years existence is probably the limit of an ephemeral publication like *Nemo's Almanac*', wrote Mrs Larden in 1894. Miss Atkinson planned 'a natural war death' for the competition in its fiftieth year, but was persuaded to carry on, since it was found 'a real help and relaxation in these difficult times'. As it enters its 100th year it is flourishing as never before. I hope these words will be echoed by its editor 100 years hence.

HOW TO USE THIS BOOK

In this book, I've tried to maintain the best Nemo traditions while introducing a much broader range of authors. I hope there will be something for everybody: one of the great pleasures of the Almanac is discovering new writers. Sometimes just because you find you really like the style of Thomas De Quincey, the approach of Katherine Mansfield or the characters of Colm Tóibín, or sometimes because the answer is such a surprise. You thought it was modern, but it turns out to be eighteenth century (or the other way around) and you go off to find more poems by Swift or Edgell Rickword; or you just fall in love with a poet and want to read more Mary Robinson or Gertrude Stein or Kathleen Jamie. And with 440 quotations rather than the usual 73, there are plenty of writers to discover in the book.

The number of quotations has meant one departure from the normal rules. In the annual Almanac no writer is quoted more than once: here, some, including Shakespeare, are quoted several times. But there are no translations. Many of the extracts can be found in the sort of chronological anthologies published by Oxford University Press and Penguin, and books of extracts and quotations on a single theme are often useful, too. One good way to start the competition is with the theme. Each month has five separate subsections, each exemplifying a single topic. Space has been left blank for you to write this in when you have identified it. Once you have the theme, you can start thinking about when each extract might have been written, and who the author might be. Old or young? Modern or earlier? Male or female? Novelist or essayist or poet? And when did people stop using that word or that phrase? It's a continuing process of narrowing down (although it's important to keep an open mind until you're sure about something) until you find the proper context and the original source. Don't expect instant answers; some will be easy to find, but others may take months. Some will be memorable and may stick in your mind as if you'd learned them by heart, others less so.

Unlike for the pamphlet form of the Almanac, most of the answers are provided here in the book. There is only one exception: each subsection has one answer, the seventh, missing, so that there are 60 answers that, should you want to, you can find entirely for yourselves. Apart from that, the book follows the same general structure as the Almanac: it is organised into twelve months, but instead of six quotations on a single theme, there are five themed subsections each containing seven quotations, of varying degrees of difficulty. There is also a short opening section, called 'Nemo's Welcome', of ten quotations, together with a matching closing section, 'Valedictory'. These do not include any unanswered questions.

The 60 seventh quotations, the ones with no answer provided, constitute a competition of their own. For more information about this, see www.nemosalmanac.com. But remember, the Nemo rules apply: don't use the internet to find the answers. It's a question of honour.

NEMO'S
WELCOME

1.

'O! Don't cut my throat, sir,' I pleaded in terror. 'Pray don't
do it, sir.'

   'Tell us your name!' said the man. 'Quick!'

   'Pip, sir.'

2.

Twice or thrice had I loved thee,
Before I knew thy face or name;
So in a voice, so in a shapelesse flame,
Angells affect us oft, and worship'd bee

3.

Gus is the Cat at the Theatre Door.
His name, as I ought to have told you before,
Is really Asparagus. That's such a fuss
To pronounce, that we usually call him just Gus.

4.

What's in a name? that which we call a rose,
By any other name would smell as sweet.

5.

Perhaps being old is having lighted rooms
Inside your head, and people in them, acting.
People you know, yet can't quite name;

6.

At length, in 1812, Mr. Williams made his début on the
stage of Ratcliffe Highway, and executed those unparalleled
murders which have procured for him such a brilliant and
undying reputation.

7.

So peaceful rests, without a stone, a name,
What once had beauty, titles, wealth, and fame.
How lov'd, how honour'd once, avails thee not,
To whom related, or by whom begot;

8.

My True Name is so well known in the Records, or Registers
at *Newgate*, and in the *Old-Baily*, and there are some things
of such Consequence still depending there, relating to my
particular Conduct, that it is not to be expected I should set
my Name, or the Account of my Family to this Work

9.

I have no name
I am but two days old.—
What shall I call thee?
I happy am
Joy is my name

10.

She was likewise my School-Mistress to teach me the
Language: When I pointed to anything, she told me the name
of it in her own Tongue, so that in a few Days I was able to call
for whatever I had a mind to. She was very good natured, and
not above forty Foot high, being little for her Age.

THE ALMANAC

JANUARY

A: _____

1.

When icicles hang by the wall
    And Dick the shepherd blows his nail,
And Tom bears logs into the hall,
    And milk comes frozen home in pail;
When blood is nipt, and ways be foul,
Then nightly sings the staring owl
    Tu-whit!
Tu-who! A merry note!
While greasy Joan doth keel the pot.

2.

Say it is ásh-boughs: whether on a December day and furled
Fast ór they in clammyish lashtender combs creep
Apart wide and new-nestle at heaven most high.
They touch heaven, tabour on it; how their talons sweep
The smouldering enormous winter welkin!

3.

Twere wholsomer for mee, that winter did
    Benight the glory of this place,
    And that a grave frost did forbid
These trees to laugh and mocke mee to my face;
    But that I may not this disgrace
Indure, nor yet leave loving, Love let mee
    Some senslesse peece of this place bee;

4.

It lay thickly drifted on the crooked crosses and headstones,
on the spears of the little gate, on the barren thorns. His soul
swooned slowly as he heard the snow falling faintly through
the universe and faintly falling, like the descent of their last
end, upon all the living and the dead.

5.

A neat, snug study on a winter's night
    A book, a friend, single lady, or a glass
Of claret, sandwich, and an appetite
Are things which make an English evening pass.

6.

O come to the window, dear brother, and see
What a change has been made in the night;
The snow has quite cover'd the broad cedar-tree,
And the bushes are sprinkled with white.

7.

They watched the stellar points come out at last in a colder
heaven, and then, shuddering a little, arm in arm, they turned
away, with a sense that the winter night was even more cruel
than the tyranny of men – turned back to drawn curtains and
a brighter fire and a glittering tea-tray and more and more talk
about the long martyrdom of women.

B: _____

1.

At Forty-ninth Street Peter turned to Dean. 'Beautiful morning,' he said gravely, squinting up his owlish eyes.

'Probably is.'

'Go get some breakfast, hey?'

Dean agreed—with additions.

'Breakfast and liquor.'

'Breakfast and liquor,' repeated Peter, and they looked at each other, nodding. 'That's logical.'

2.

The divine took his seat at the breakfast-table, and began to compose his spirits by the gentle sedative of a large cup of tea, the demulcent of a well-buttered muffin, and the tonic of a small lobster.

3.

I catched a good big catfish, too, and Jim cleaned him with his knife, and fried him.

When breakfast was ready we lolled on the grass and eat it smoking hot. Jim laid it in with all his might, for he was most about starved. Then when we had got pretty well stuffed, we laid off and lazied.

4.

H— proposed that we should have scrambled eggs for breakfast. He said he would cook them. It seemed, from his account, that he was very good at doing scrambled eggs. He often did them at picnics and when out on yachts. He was quite famous for them. People who had once tasted his scrambled eggs, so we gathered from his conversation, never cared for any other food afterwards, but pined away and died when they could not get them.

5.

The tea consumed was the very best, the coffee the very blackest, the cream the very thickest; there was dry toast and buttered toast, muffins and crumpets; hot bread and cold bread, white bread and brown bread, home-made bread and bakers' bread, wheaten bread and oaten bread; and if there be other breads than these, they were there.

6.

You cannot eat breakfast all day,
Nor is it the act of a sinner,
When breakfast is taken away,
To turn his attention to dinner;

7.

Then to his music; and his song
Tastes of his breakfast all day long.

C: _____

1.

They were aching with fatigue and bruised with tumbles; they had fallen into several holes and got wet through; the snow was getting so deep that they could hardly drag their little legs through it, and the trees were thicker and more like each other than ever.

2.

When men were all asleep the snow came flying,
In large white flakes falling on the city brown,
Stealthily and perpetually settling and loosely lying,
Hushing the latest traffic of the drowsy town;

3.

One must have a mind of winter
To regard the frost and the boughs
Of the pine-trees crusted with snow;

4.

Whose woods these are I think I know.
His house is in the village though;
He will not see me stopping here
To watch his woods fill up with snow.

5.

Snow had fallen, snow on snow,
Snow on snow,
In the bleak mid-winter
Long ago.

6.

Monday. — Here's a day! The ground covered with snow!
What is to become of us? We were to have walked out early
to near shops, and had the carriage for the more distant.
Mr. Richard Snow is dreadfully fond of us. I dare say he has
stretched himself out at Chawton too.

7.

It was January. Snow was falling; snow had fallen all day. The
sky spread like a grey goose's wing from which feathers were
falling all over England. The sky was nothing but a flurry of
falling flakes. Lanes were levelled; hollows filled; the snow
clogged the streams; obscured windows, and lay wedged
against doors.

D: _____

1.

> All shod with steel,
> We hissed along the polished ice in games
> Confederate, imitative of the chase
> And woodland pleasures

2.

There was also the newer fashion of skating—figure-skating: Hatty pointed it out to Tom. In one place an orange had been set centrally upon the ice, and four top-hatted, dignified gentlemen were describing a harmony of figures to it—from it,—round it. Suddenly a town-urchin, on rusty Fen-runners, partly strapped, partly tied with string to his boots, dashed in, snatched up the orange and dashed away again with his teeth already in it.

3.

But the skater came closer. Legs, hands, carriage, were a boy's, but no boy ever had a mouth like that; no boy had those breasts; no boy had eyes which looked as if they had been fished from the bottom of the sea. Finally, coming to a stop and sweeping a curtsey with the utmost grace to the King, who was shuffling past on the arm of some Lord-in-waiting, the unknown skater came to a standstill.

4.

> Or where the lake
> And long canal the cerule plain extend,
> The city pours her thousands, swarming all,
> From every quarter; and, with him who slides;
> Or skating sweeps, swift as the winds, along,

In circling poise; or else disorder'd falls,
His feet, illuded, sprawling to the sky,
While the laugh rages round;

5.

Having seene the strange, and wonderfull dexterity of the
sliders on the new Canall in St. James's Park perform'd by divers
Gent: & others with *Scheets*, after the manner of the *Hollanders*,
with what pernicitie & swiftnesse they passe, how sudainly
they stop in full carriere upon the Ice, before their *Majesties*:
I went home by water but not without exceeding difficultie,
The *Thames* being frozen, great flakes of yce incompassing
our boate.

6.

The skaters were moving like space voyagers in the void of
whiteness; their cries and their shouts and their laughter
thrummed, magnified in the silence as if the low, white sky
were padded with soundproofing cloud. The stone college
buildings across the lawn that shelved down to the river
seemed discoloured ivory against the blazing whiteness of
the snowladen scene.

7.

Smile, Death, as you fasten the blades to my feet for me,
On, on let us skate past the sleeping willows dusted with
    snow;
Fast, fast down the frozen stream, with the moor and the
    road and the vision behind

E: _____

1.

There was a Boy whose name was Jim;
His Friends were very good to him.
They gave him Tea, and Cakes, and Jam,
And slices of delicious Ham,
And Chocolate with pink inside

2.

He weeps by the side of the ocean,
    He weeps on the top of the hill;
He purchases pancakes and lotion,
    And chocolate shrimps from the mill.

3.

'You can take your bloody prize,' Bill said, 'and hop it. What
do you want? Chocolates?'
    'I don't eat chocolates,' the Boy said.

4.

Thus daily his gouty inventions he pained,
  And all for to save the expenses of brickbat;
That engine so fatal, which Denham had brained,
  And too much resembled his wife's chocolate.

5.

He walked round the shop with a conscious swagger, pausing to pop into his mouth a Butter Ball—composed, as the label stated, of pure farm cream and best butter. It was all his—all those rows and rows of gleaming bottles of sweets of every size and colour, those boxes and boxes of attractively arranged chocolates. Deliberately he imagined himself as their owner. By the time he had walked round the shop three times he believed that he was the owner.

6.

Waked in the morning with my head in a sad taking through the last night's drink, which I am very sorry for; so rose, and went with Mr Creed to drink our morning draught which he did give me in Chocolate to settle my stomach.

7.

I like your chocolate, good Mistress Fry!
I like your cookery in every way;
I like your shrove-tide service and supply;
I like to hear your sweet *Pandeans* play;
I like the pity in your full-brimm'd eye;
I like your carriage, and your silken grey,
Your dove-like habits, and your silent preaching;
But I don't like your Newgatory teaching.

FEBRUARY

A: _____

1.

I wish I lived in a caravan,
With a horse to drive, like the pedlar man!
Where he comes from nobody knows,
Or where he goes to, but on he goes!

2.

There is a hotel in Gatwick airport where you could live for the
rest of your life. You could stay there until they found you, and
they would never find you — why should they? You could eat
the stale croissants from trays set out in the hallways, wash
out your smalls in the sink, nip from room to room when the
cleaning trolley went round.

3.

You were fast asleep at Crewe and so you never knew
That he was walking up and down the station;
You were sleeping all the while he was busy at Carlisle,
Where he greets the stationmaster with elation.
But you saw him at Dumfries, where he speaks to the police
If there's anything they ought to know about:

4.

Amar was running after the car. It was still there, ahead of
him, going further away and faster. He could never catch it,
but he ran because there was nothing else to do. And as he ran,
his sandals made a terrible flapping noise on the hard surface
of the highway, and he kicked them off, and ran silently and
with freedom. Now for a moment he had the exultant feeling
of flying along the road behind the car.

5.

For like a mole I journey in the dark,
    A-travelling along the underground
From my Pillar'd Halls and broad Suburbean Park,
    To come the daily dull official round;
And home again at night with my pipe all alight,
    A-scheming how to count ten bob a pound.

6.

Before the Roman came to Rye or out to Severn strode,
The rolling English drunkard made the rolling English road.
A rolling road, a reeling road, it rambles round the shire,
And after him the parson ran, the sexton and the squire;
A merry road, a mazy road, and such as we did tread
The night we went to Birmingham by way of Beachy Head.

7.

I don't suppose they had ever thought about railways except as
a means of getting to Maskelyne and Cook's, the Pantomime,
Zoological Gardens, and Madame Tussaud's. They were just
ordinary suburban children, and they lived with their Father
and Mother in an ordinary red-brick-fronted villa, with
coloured glass in the front door.

B: _____

1.

The fog grew thicker; she looked up at the windows beneath the dome and saw that they were a dusky yellow. Then her eye discerned an official walking along the upper gallery, and in pursuance of her grotesque humour, her mocking misery, she likened him to a black, lost soul, doomed to wander in an eternity of vain research along endless shelves.

2.

Fog everywhere. Fog up the river, where it flows among green aits and meadows; fog down the river, where it rolls defiled among the tiers of shipping, and the waterside pollutions of a great (and dirty) city. Fog on the Essex marshes, fog on the Kentish heights. Fog creeping into the cabooses of collier-brigs; fog lying out on the yards, and hovering in the rigging of great ships; fog drooping on the gunwales of barges and small boats.

3.

"What sort of a place is it, Morgan?" asked the Major, out of the bed-curtains in Bury Street the next morning, as the valet was arranging his toilette in the deep yellow London fog.

4.

Nearly a year later, in the month of October 18—, London was startled by a crime of singular ferocity and rendered all the more notable by the high position of the victim. The details were few and startling. A maid servant living alone in a house not far from the river, had gone upstairs to bed about eleven. Although a fog rolled over the city in the small hours, the early part of the night was cloudless, and the lane, which the maid's window overlooked, was brilliantly lit by the full moon

5.

"It may be only blackmail," said the man in the taxi hopefully.
The fog was like a saffron blanket soaked in ice-water. It had
hung over London all day and at last was beginning to descend.
The sky was yellow as a duster and the rest was a granular
black, overprinted in grey and lightened by occasional slivers
of bright fish colour as a policeman turned in his wet cape.

6.

She walked on through the fog into Tottenham Court Road.
The houses and the people passing were withdrawn, nebulous.
There was only a grey fog shot with yellow lights, and its cold
breath on her face, and the ghost of herself coming out of the
fog to meet her.

7.

An omnibus across the bridge
    Crawls like a yellow butterfly,
    And, here and there, a passer-by
Shows like a little restless midge.

Big barges full of yellow hay
    Are moved against the shadowy wharf,
    And, like a yellow silken scarf,
The thick fog hangs along the quay.

C: _____

1.

>   Aye, there's the rub,
> For in that sleep of death what dreams may come
> When we have shuffled off this mortal coil
> Must give us pause.

2.

> Like sylvan nymphs my pages shall be clad;
> My men, like satyrs grazing on the lawns,
> Shall with their goat-feet dance an antic hay.

3.

> Ask for this great Deliverer now, and find him
> Eyeless in *Gaza* at the Mill with slaves,
> Himself in bonds under Philistian yoke.

4.

> The woods decay, the woods decay and fall,
> The vapours weep their burthen to the ground,
> Man comes and tills the field and lies beneath,
> And after many a summer dies the swan.

5.

> O, wonder!
> How many goodly creatures are there here!
> How beauteous mankind is! O brave new world,
> That has such people in't!

6.

Sweet is the lore which Nature brings;
Our meddling intellect
Mis-shapes the beauteous forms of things:—
We murder to dissect.

Enough of Science and of Art;
Close up those barren leaves;
Come forth, and bring with you a heart
That watches and receives.

7.

But first the notion that man has a body distinct from his
soul, is to be expunged; this I shall do, by printing in the
infernal method, by corrosives, which in Hell are salutary and
medicinal, melting apparent surfaces away, and displaying
the infinite which was hid.

If the doors of perception were cleansed every thing would
appear to man as it is: infinite.

For man has closed himself up, till he sees all things thro'
narrow chinks of his cavern.

D: _____

1.

Crist have mercy on me and foryeve me my giltes; and namely of my translaciouns and enditynges of worldly vanitees, the whiche I revoke in my retracciouns: as is the book of Troilus; the book also of Fame; the book of the XXV. Ladies; the book of the Duchesse; the book of Seint Valentynes day of the Parlement of Briddes...

2.

For on a day when *Cupid* kept his court,
    As he is wont at each Saint Valentide,
    Unto the which all lovers doe resort,
That of their loves successe they there may make report;

3.

Here is the nosegay — how simple it shines,
    It speaks without words, to the ear and the eye:
The flowers of the spring, are the best Valentines,
    They are young, fair, and simple, and pleasingly shy.
That you may remain so, and ne'er act contrary,
I send you these flowers, as a Valentine Mary.

4.

Oft have I heard both Youths and Virgins say,
Birds chuse their Mates, and couple too, this day:
But by their flight I never can divine,
When shall I couple with my Valentine.

5.

To morrow is Saint Valentine's day,
    All in the morning betime,
And I a maid at your window,
    To be your Valentine.
Then up he rose, and donn'd his clo'es,
    And dupp'd the chamber door,
Let in the maid that out a maid
    Never departed more.

6.

"I—I didn't—I know I ought never to have dreamt of sending
that valentine—forgive me, sir—it was a wanton thing which
no woman with any self-respect should have done. If you will
only pardon my thoughtlessness, I promise never to— "

"No, no, no. Don't say thoughtlessness! Make me think
it was something more—that it was a sort of prophetic
instinct—the beginning of a feeling that you would like me.
You torture me to say it was done in thoughtlessness."

7.

A fellow that lives in a windmill has not a more whimsical
dwelling than the heart of a man that is lodged in a woman.
There is no point of the compass to which they cannot turn,
and by which they are not turned; and by one as well as
another, for motion, not method is their occupation. To know
this, and yet continue to be in love, is to be made wise from
the dictates of reason, and yet persevere to play the fool by
the force of instinct. — Oh, here come my pair
of turtles. — What, billing so sweetly? Is not
Valentine's day over with you yet?

E: _____

I.

The silver Swan, who living had no Note,
When Death approcht, unlockt her silent throat;
Leaning her brest against the reedy shore,
Thus sung her first and last, and sung no more:
Farewell all joyes; O Death, come close mine eyes;
More Geese then Swans now live, more fooles then wise.

2.

A sudden blow: the great wings beating still
Above the staggering girl, her thighs caressed
By the dark webs, her nape caught in his bill,

3.

The death of the Squire was not the death of the church,
though they drew to their end together. He died, and the Big
House was sold by auction and became a Home for Invalids.
The lake silted up, the swans flew away, and the great pike
choked in the reeds. With the Squire's hand removed, we fell
apart — though we were about to do so anyway.

4.

With that I saw two Swannes of goodly hewe,
Come softly swimming downe along the Lee;
Two fairer Birds I yet did never see:
The snow which doth the top of *Pindus* strew,
Did never whiter shew,
Nor Jove himselfe when he a Swan would be
For love of Leda, whiter did appeare:

5.

Through the dark robe oft amber rays prevail,
    And like fair veins in sable marble flow;
Still warble, dying swan! still tell the tale,
    The enchanting tale, the tale of pleasing woe.

6.

While the great swan with slow and creaking flight
Went slanting down towards safety, where the stream
Shines through the trees below, with glance and gleam
Of blue aerial eyes that seem to give
Sense to the sightless earth and make it live.

7.

I never eat a bit of a Swan before, and I think it good eating
with sweet sauce. The Swan was killed 3 weeks before it was
eat and yet not the least bad taste in it.

MARCH

A: _____

1.

Diego had no sooner opened the door, than he cried out, and
ran back—I ran back too, and said, Is it the ghost? The ghost!
No, no, said Diego, and his hair stood on end—it is a giant,
I believe; he is clad all in armour, for I saw his foot and part
of his leg, and they are as large as the helmet below in the
court.

2.

But the ghost sat down on the opposite side of the fireplace,
as if he were quite used to it.

'You don't believe in me,' observed the Ghost.

'I don't,' said —.

3.

Each Ghost must act a proper part,
Observe *Decorum*'s needful grace,
And keep the laws of *Time* and *Place*;
Must change, with happy variation,
His manners with his situation;
What in the country might pass down,
Would be impertinent in town.

4.

I gathered that what he chiefly remembers about it is a
horrible, an intensely horrible, face of *crumpled linen*. What
expression he read upon it he could not or would not tell, but
that the fear of it went nigh to maddening him is certain.

5.

I rose, and endeavoured to unhasp the casement. The hook was soldered into the staple: a circumstance observed by me when awake, but forgotten. 'I must stop it, nevertheless!' I muttered, knocking my knuckles through the glass, and stretching an arm out to seize the importunate branch: instead of which, my fingers closed on the fingers of a little, ice-cold hand!

6.

This is not a story to pass on.

Down by the stream in back of 124 her footprints come and go, come and go. They are so familiar. Should a child, an adult place his feet in them, they will fit. Take them out and they disappear again as though nobody ever walked there.

By and by all trace is gone, and what is forgotten is not only the footprints but the water too and what is down there.

7.

The apparition had reached the landing half way up and was therefore on the spot nearest the window, where, at sight of me, it stopped short and fixed me exactly as it had fixed me from the tower and from the garden. He knew me as well as I knew him; and so, in the cold, faint twilight, with a glimmer in the high glass and another on the polish of the oak stair below, we faced each other in our common intensity. He was absolutely, on this occasion, a living, detestable, dangerous presence.

B: _____

1.

Or, as the snail, whose tender horns being hit,
Shrinks backward in his shelly cave with pain,
And there, all smother'd up, in shade doth sit,
Long after fearing to come forth again:
    So, at his bloody view, her eyes are fled
    Into the deep dark cabins of her head.

2.

Jet-black and shining, from the dripping hedge
Slow peeps the fearful snail,
    And from each tiny bent
    Withdraws his timid horn

3.

He had taken no trouble to indicate it to his fellow citizens,
purveyors and consumers, in his own and the circumjacent
commonwealths, of comic matter in large lettering, diurnally
'set up', printed, published, folded and delivered, at the
expense of his presumptuous emulation of the snail. The
snail had become for him, under this ironic suggestion, the
loveliest beast in nature, and his return to England, of which
we are present witnesses, hadn't been unconnected with the
appreciation so determined.

4.

I own my humble life, good friend;
Snail was I born, and snail shall end.
And what's a butterfly? At best,
He's but a caterpillar, drest:

5.

'Will you walk a little faster?' said a whiting to a snail,
'There's a porpoise close behind us, and he's treading
    on my tail.'

6.

'I'm going out to buy a newspaper.'
    'Yes?'
    'Though it's no good buying newspapers.... Nothing ever
happens. Curse this war; God damn this war!... All the same,
I don't see why we should have a snail on our wall.'
    Ah, the mark on the wall! It was a snail.

7.

The shell of a little snail bleached
In the grass; chip of flint, and mite
Of chalk; and the small birds' dung
In splashes of purest white:

C: _____

1.

I can't help suspecting, that there is, or may be, some regurgitation from the bath into the cistern of the pump. In that case, what a delicate beveridge is every day quaffed by the drinkers; medicated with the sweat and dirt, and dandriff; and the abominable discharges of various kinds, from twenty different diseased bodies, parboiling in the kettle below.

2.

Behold me waiting — waiting for the knife.
A little while, and at a leap I storm
The thick, sweet mystery of chloroform,
The drunken dark, the little-death-in-life.

3.

I have in this one dirty business of Laudanum an hundred times deceived, tricked, nay, actually & consciously LIED. — And yet *all* these vices are so opposite to my nature, that but for this *free-agency-annihilating Poison*, I verily believe that I should have suffered myself to be cut in pieces rather than have committed any one of them.

4.

Provident junkies, known as squirrels, keep stashes against a bust. Every time I take a shot I let a few drops fall in my vast pocket, the lining is stiff with stuff. I had a plastic dropper in my shoe and a safety-pin stuck in my belt.

5.

> Not poppy, nor mandragora,
> Nor all the drowsy syrups of the world,
> Shall ever medicine thee to that sweet sleep
> Which thou owedst yesterday.

6.

The pleasure given by wine is always mounting, and tending to a crisis, after which it declines: that from opium, when once generated, is stationary for eight or ten hours: the first, to borrow a technical distinction from medicine, is a case of acute — the second, of chronic pleasure: the one is a flame, the other a steady and equable glow. But the main distinction lies in this, that whereas wine disorders the mental faculties, opium, on the contrary (if taken in a proper manner), introduces amongst them the most exquisite order, legislation, and harmony.

7.

So much has romanticism debauched us, that, without some form of vagueness, we deny the highest. In the classic it is always the light of ordinary day, never the light that never was on land or sea. It is always perfectly human and never exaggerated: man is always man and never a god. But the awful result of romanticism is that, accustomed to this strange light, you can never live without it. Its effect on you is that of a drug.

D: _____

1.

I have forgot much, Cynara! gone with the wind,
Flung roses, roses riotously with the throng

2.

      Mighty winds
That sweep the skirt of some far-spreading wood
Of ancient growth, make music not unlike
The dash of Ocean on his winding shore.

3.

O wild West Wind, thou breath of Autumn's being,
Thou, from whose unseen presence the leaves dead
Are driven, like ghosts from an enchanter fleeing,

4.

Tonight the winds begin to rise
    And roar from yonder dropping day:
    The last red leaf is whirl'd away,
The rooks are blown about the skies.

5.

What a wind! Whooping and banging all along the street, the kind of wind that blows everything topsy-turvy.

    Seventy-five, today, and a topsy-turvy day of wind and sunshine. The kind of wind that gets into the blood and drives you wild. Wild!

    And I give a little shiver because suddenly I know, I know it in my ancient water, that something will happen today.

6.

Not I, not I, but the wind that blows through me!
A fine wind is blowing the new direction of Time.
If only I let it bear me, carry me, if only it carry me!
If only I am sensitive, subtle, oh, delicate, a winged gift!

7.

There is no obstacle
But Gregory's wood and one bare hill
Whereby the haystack- and roof-levelling wind,
Bred on the Atlantic, can be stayed.

E: _____

1.

I love to recall the glad monotony of a Pacific voyage, when the trades are not stinted and the ship, day after day, goes free. The mountain scenery of trade-wind clouds, watched (and in my case painted) under every vicissitude of light— blotting stars, withering in the moon's glory, barring the scarlet eve, lying across the dawn collapsed into the unfeatured morning bank

2.

And the stately ships go on
    To their haven under the hill;
But O for the touch of a vanish'd hand,
    And the sound of a voice that is still!

3.

'Believe me, my young friend, there is NOTHING—absolutely nothing—half so much worth doing as simply messing about in boats. Simply messing,' he went on dreamily: 'messing— about—in—boats; messing—'

4.

The boat reappeared—but brother and sister had gone down in one embrace never to be parted: living through again in one supreme moment, the days when they had clasped their little hands in love, and roamed the daisied fields together.

5.

Some years ago—never mind how long precisely—having little or no money in my purse, and nothing particular to interest me on shore, I thought I would sail about a little and see the watery part of the world.

6.

The histories of schooners
Are murmured in coral,
Their cargoes of sponges
On sandspits of islets
Barques white as white salt
Of acrid Saint Maarten,
Hulls crusted with barnacles,
Holds foul with great turtles

7.

I was near two Months performing this last Work, *viz.*
rigging and fitting my Mast and Sails; for I finish'd them very
compleat, making a small Stay, and a Sail, or Foresail to it, to
assist, if we should turn to Windward; and which was more
than all, I fix'd a Rudder to the Stern of her, to steer with;

APRIL

A: _____

1.

April is the cruellest month, breeding
Lilacs out of the dead land,

2.

When April scatters coins of primrose gold
Among the copper leaves in thickets old,
And singing skylarks from the meadows rise,
To twinkle like black stars in sunny skies.

3.

What gentle ghost, besprent with April dew,
    Hails me so solemnly to yonder yew,
And beckoning woos me, from the fatal tree
    To pluck a garland for herself, or me?

4.

Oh, to be in England
Now that April's there,
And whoever wakes in England
Sees, some morning, unaware,
That the lowest boughs and the brushwood sheaf
Round the elm-tree bole are in tiny leaf,

5.

Whan that Aprille with hir shoures soote
The droghte of Merche hath perced to the roote

6.

Cleare or cloudie sweet as Aprill showring,
Smoth or frowning So is hir face to mee,
Pleasd or smiling like milde May all flowring,
When skies blew silke and medowes carpets bee,

7.

Why are you vext Ladie, why doe you frowne?
Here dwell no frowns, nor anger, from these gates
Sorrow flies farre: see here be all the pleasurs
That fancie can beget on youthfull thoughts
When the fresh blood grows lively, and returns
Brisk as the April buds in primrose season.

B: _____

1.

—"Are we not here now;"—continued the Corporal—"and are we not,"—dropping his hat plumb upon the ground—and pausing, before he pronounced the word,—"gone! in a moment?" The descent of the hat was as if a heavy lump of clay had been kneaded into the crown of it.—Nothing could have expressed the sentiment of mortality, of which it was the type and forerunner, like it;

2.

For his Hat was a hundred and two feet wide,
With ribbons and bibbons on every side
And bells, and buttons, and loops, and lace,
So that nobody ever could see the face

3.

I must have looked aghast, but he seemed to think he had done rather well. There was a hint of a smile on his face. He also appeared to have decided that the examination was over and started to look around for his hat. He reached out his hand and took hold of his wife's head, tried to lift it off, to put it on.

4.

Six years older, shorter, wider, with breasts on her belly and no hair (though she took the peculiar step of putting her wig in curlers) and slippers just visible under a long, padded baby-pink housecoat. But the real difference was. Hortense was eighty-four.

5.

With varying vanities, from every part,
They shift the moving toyshop of their heart,
Where wigs with wigs, with sword-knots sword-knots strive,
Beaux banish beaux, and coaches coaches drive.

6.

He brought back a knife. Unsheathed, it smiled at me, curving up in a grin.

He took the hat from my mouth.
'Tell me you love me,' he said.
Gently, I did.
The end came anyway.

7.

'Look, she made me this bow to my hat, and put in the feather last night. There now, you are going to laugh at me too. But why should not I wear pink ribbons? I do not care if it is the Doctor's favourite colour.'

C: _____

1.

I tried to say, "The death she has died, Sergeant, was a death of her own seeking." No! the words wouldn't come. The dumb trembling held me in its grip. I couldn't feel the driving rain. I couldn't see the rising tide. As in the vision of a dream, the poor lost creature came back before me. I saw her again as I had seen her in the past time—on the morning when I went to fetch her into the house. I heard her again, telling me that the Shivering Sand seemed to draw her to it against her will,

2.

This small lake was of most value as a neighbor in the intervals of a gentle rain storm in August, when, both air and water being perfectly still, but the sky overcast, mid-afternoon had all the serenity of evening, and the wood-thrush sang around, and was heard from shore to shore.

3.

Flora was fair, and blooming as that flower
Which spreads its blossom to the April shower;
Her gentle manners and unstudied grace
Still added lustre to her beaming face,
While every look, by purity refined,
Displayed the lovelier beauties of her mind.

4.

Then the clouds opened and let down the rain like a waterfall. The water bounded from the mountain-top, tore leaves and branches from the trees, poured like a cold shower over the struggling heap on the sand. Presently the heap broke up and figures staggered away. Only the beast lay still, a few yards from the sea. Even in the rain they could see how small a beast it was; and already its blood was staining the sand.

5.
I shall not see the shadows,
    I shall not feel the rain;
I shall not hear the nightingale
    Sing on, as if in pain:

6.
    And sometimes too a burst of rain,
Swept from the black horizon, broad, descends
In one continuous flood. Still over head
The mingling tempest weaves its gloom, and still
The deluge deepens; till the fields around
Lie sunk, and flatted, in the sordid wave.

7.
There's a mountain of blackness in the sky, and the greatest rain falling has been these long years on the earth. The gods help Conchubor. He'll be a sorry man this night, reaching his dun, and he with all his spirits, thinking to himself he'll be putting his arms around her in two days or three.

D: _____

1.

There are two beds, a big one for madame and a smaller one on the opposite side for monsieur. The wash-basin is shut off by a curtain. It is a large room, the smell of cheap hotels faint, almost imperceptible. The street outside is narrow, cobble-stoned, going sharply uphill and ending in a flight of steps. What they call an impasse.

2.

Dear Paris of the hot white hands, the scarlet lips, the
    scented hair,
Une jolie fille à vendre, très cher;
A thing of gaiety, a thing of sorrow,
Bought tonight, possessed, and tossed
Back to the mart again to-morrow.

3.

He had pulled down the green baize blind, and was looking over the roofs and chimney-pots of Paris and all about with all his eyes, munching the while a roll and a savoury saveloy, in which there was evidence of much garlic. He ate with great relish, for he had been all morning at Carrel's studio, drawing from the life.

4.

If I rightly remember, it happened on that afternoon when
Word of the nearer approach of a new Neapolitan army
First was spread. I began to bethink me of Paris Septembers,
Thought I could fancy the look of that old 'Ninety-two. On
    that evening
Three or four, or, it may be, five, of these people were
    slaughtered.

5.

Paris rawly waking, crude sunlight on her lemon streets. Moist pith of farls of bread, the froggreen wormwood, her matin incense, court the air. Belluomo rises from the bed of his wife's lover's wife, the kerchiefed housewife is astir, a saucer of acetic acid in her hands. In Rodot's Yvonne and Madeleine newmake their tumbled beauties,

6.

Long petticoats to hide the feet,
    Silk hose with clocks of scarlet;
A load of perfume, sick'ning sweet,
    Bought of Parisian varlet.

7.

She bid me adieu twice – I repeated it as often; and so cordial was the parting between us, that had it happen'd any where else, I'm not sure but I should have signed it with a kiss of charity, as warm and holy as an apostle.

But in Paris, as none kiss each other but the men — I did, what amounted to the same thing —

— I bid God bless her.

E: _____

1.

Even working in a library for two years had not lessened her love of reading. There was *Frenchman's Creek*. She stopped for a second, remembering the glamour of the Frenchman. If only a man like that would come into the library. But if he did, he'd be bound to fall in love with Gloria.

A commotion at the issue desk woke her out of her reverie. A man with a moustache and a purple face, wearing a blazer, was agitatedly waving a copy of Molly Parkin's latest novel.

'It's filth,' he roared, 'sheer filth.'

2.

A small breakfast-room adjoined the drawing-room: I slipped in there. It contained a book-case: I soon possessed myself of a volume, taking care that it should be one stored with pictures. I mounted into the window-seat: gathering up my feet, I sat cross-legged, like a Turk; and, having drawn the red moreen curtain nearly close, I was shrined in double retirement.

3.

The Way I read a Letter's – this –
'Tis first – I lock the Door –
And push it with my fingers – next –
For transport it be sure –

4.

But from fifteen to seventeen she was in training for a heroine; she read all such works as heroines must read to supply their memories with those quotations which are so serviceable and so soothing in the vicissitudes of their eventful lives.

5.

I'm reading with the light on
    though it's 4 o'clock in the afternoon
and the skylight overhead, masked
    with a calico blind, casts
a whiteness in the air as if a blanket
    of snow had covered the pane
and light was filtering through flakes.

6.

The bookful blockhead, ignorantly read,
With loads of learned lumber in his head,
With his own tongue still edifies his ears,
And always list'ning to himself appears.
All books he reads, and all he reads assails,
From Dryden's Fables down to Durfey's Tales.

7

'Why then,' said the medical gentleman, 'there are hopes
for me yet; I may attend half the old women in Bristol if I've
decent luck. Get out, you mouldy old villain, get out.' With
this adjuration, which was addressed to the large book, the
medical gentleman kicked the volume with remarkable
agility to the further end of the shop, and pulling off his
green spectacles, grinned the identical grin of Robert Sawyer,
Esquire, formerly of Guy's Hospital in the Borough, with a
private residence in Lant-street.

MAY

A: _____

1.

When us was wed she turned afraid
Of love and me and all things human;
Like the shut of a winter's day
Her smile went out, and 'twasn't a woman —
    More like a little frightened fay.

2.

My true love hath my heart, and I have his,
By just exchange, one for the other giv'n.
I hold his dear, and mine he cannot miss:
There never was a better bargain driv'n.

3.

The Stage is more beholding to love, than the life of Man. For
as to the Stage, love is ever a matter of comedies, and now
and then of tragedies: but in life, it doth much mischief:
sometimes like a Siren; sometimes like a Fury.

4.

But love is a durable fire
    In the mind ever burning;
Never sick, never old, never dead,
    From itself never turning.

5.

But the symptoms of the mind in lovers are almost infinite,
and so diverse, that no art can comprehend them; though
they be merry sometimes, and rapt beyond themselves for joy;
yet most part love is a plague, a torture, a hell, a bitter sweet
passion at last;

6.

When I am sad and weary
When I think all hope has gone,
When I walk along High Holborn
I think of you with nothing on.

7.

If I worship one thing more than another it shall be the
    spread of my own body, or any part of it,
Translucent mould of me it shall be you!
Shaded ledges and rests it shall be you!
Firm masculine colter it shall be you!

B: _____

1.

They arrived at twilight, and, as we strolled out among the sparkling hundreds, Daisy's voice was playing murmurous tricks in her throat.

'These things excite me so,' she whispered. 'If you want to kiss me any time during the evening, Nick, just let me know and I'll be glad to arrange it for you. Just mention my name. Or present a green card. I'm giving out green—'

2.

Gin a body meet a body
     Comin thro' the glen;
Gin a body kiss a body,
     Need the warld ken!

3.

But his naïveté made people protective, and women were drawn by his innocence. They wanted to wrap their arms around him or something, so lost and boyish did he look at times. Not that this was entirely uncontrived, or unexploited. When I was small and the two of us sat in Lyon's Cornerhouse drinking milkshakes, he'd send me like a messenger pigeon to women at other tables, and have me announce, 'My daddy wants to give you a kiss.'

4.

On thy withered Lips and dry,
Which like barren Furrows lye;
Brooding Kisses I will pour,
Shall thy youthful Heart restore.

5.

    Such kisses as belong to early days,
Where heart, and soul, and sense, in concert move,
    And the blood's lava, and the pulse a blaze,
Each kiss a heart-quake, — for a kiss's strength,
I think, it must be reckon'd by its length.

6.

Say I'm weary, say I'm sad,
Say that health and wealth have miss'd me,
Say I'm growing old, but add,
Jenny kiss'd me.

7.

Thanked be fortune it hath been otherwise
Twenty times better, but once in special,
In thin array after a pleasant guise,
When her loose gown from her shoulders did fall
And she me caught in her arms long and small,
Therewithal sweetly did me kiss
And softly said, 'Dear heart, how like you this?'

C: _____

1.

It is a truth universally acknowledged, that a single man in possession of a good fortune, must be in want of a wife.

2.

'Darling, is that you? I've got something rather awful to tell you.'
   'Yes?'
   'You'll be furious.'
   'Well?'
   'I'm engaged to be married.'
   'Who to?'
   'I hardly think I can tell you.'

3.

She was a worthy womman al hir lyve:
Housbondes at chirche dore she hadde fyve.

4.

Reader I married him.

5.

Reader I married her.

6.

Reader I married him/her.

7.

I was ever of opinion, that the honest man who married and brought up a large family, did more service than he who continued single, and only talked of population. From this motive, I had scarce taken orders a years before I began to think seriously of matrimony, and chose my wife as she did her wedding gown, not for a fine glossy surface, but such qualities as would wear well.

D: _____

1.

Then a similar ball leapt into the air and fell on the grass, where after a moment it lay still. The Bishop went as near as he dared to it, and saw—what but the remains of an enormous spider, veinous and seared! And, as the fire burned lower down, more terrible bodies like this began to break out from the trunk, and it was seen that these were covered with greyish hair.

2.

I heard a spider
and a fly arguing
wait said the fly
do not eat me
I serve a great purpose
in the world

3.

O spiders, spiders, spiders, those aristocrats of the creepy-crawly world, he had never ceased to love them, but he had somehow betrayed them from the start. He had never found an *eresus niger*, though as a boy his certainty of finding one had seemed to come direct from God. His projected book on *The Mechanics of the Orb Web* had turned into an article.

4.

The Spider as an Artist
Has never been employed —
Though his surpassing Merit
Is freely certified

5.

The most prominent object was a long table with a tablecloth spread on it, as if a feast had been in preparation when the house and the clocks all stopped together. An epergne or centre-piece of some kind was in the middle of this cloth; it was so heavily overhung with cobwebs that its form was quite undistinguishable; and, as I looked along the yellow expanse out of which I remember its seeming to grow, like a black fungus, I saw speckle-legged spiders with blotchy bodies running home to it, and running out from it, as if some circumstances of the greatest public importance had just transpired in the spider community.

6.

There may be in the cup
A spider steep'd, and one may drink, depart,
And yet partake no venom, for his knowledge
Is not infected: but if one present
The abhorr'd ingredient to his eye, make known
How he hath drunk, he cracks his gorge, his sides,
With violent hefts. I have drunk, and seen the spider.

7.

The worst Fate Bookes have, when they are once read,
They're laid aside, forgotten like the Dead:
Under a heap of dust they buried lye,
Within a vault of some small Library.
But Spiders they, for honour of that Art
Of Spinning, which by Nature they were taught;
Since Men doe spin their Writings from the Braine,
Striving to make a lasting Web of Fame,
Of Cobwebs thin, high Altars doe they raise,
There offer Flyes, as sacrifice of praise.

E: _____

1.

Oh, for the wonder that bubbles into my soul,
I would be a good fountain, a good well-head,
Would blur no whisper, spoil no expression.

2.

'It struck me as a possibility that there might be newts in
the fountain, and knowing how keen Gussie is on newts, I
advised him to wade in and hunt around.'

'With all his clothes on?'

'Yes, he had his clothes on. I remember noticing.'

'But you can't go wading in the Trafalgar Square fountain
with all your clothes on.'

'Yes, you can. Gussie did.'

3.

What are we doing when we toss a coin,
just a 5p-piece into the shallow dish
of the fountain in the city-centre
shopping arcade?

4.

That is the Ocean, our Affections here
Are but streams borrow'd from the Fountain there.
And 'tis the noblest Argument to prove
A Beauteous mind, that it knows how to Love:
Those kind Impressions which Fate can't controul,
Are Heaven's mintage on a worthy Soul.

5.

'Allay,' he cried gaily, and off they went.

Off they went, spanking along lightly, under the green and gold shade of the plane trees, through the small streets that smelled of lemons and fresh coffee, past the fountain square where women, with water-pots lifted, stopped talking to gaze after them, round the corner past the café, with its pink and white umbrellas, green tables, and blue siphons, and so to the sea front.

6.

His Love no Modesty allows:
By swift degrees advancing where
His daring Hand that Alter seiz'd,
Where Gods of Love do Sacrifice;
That awful Throne, that Paradise,
Where Rage is tam'd, and Anger pleas'd;
That Living Fountain, from whose Trills
The melted Soul in liquid Drops distils.

7.

And, after all, it was as magnificent a piece of work as ever human skill contrived. At the foot of the palatial facade was strown, with careful art and ordered irregularity, a broad and broken heap of massive rock, looking as if it might have lain there since the deluge. Over a central precipice fell the water, in a semicircular cascade; and from a hundred crevices on all sides, snowy jets gushed up, and streams spouted out of the mouths and nostrils of stone monsters, and fell in glistening drops;

JUNE

A: _____

1.

Sol thro' white Curtains shot a tim'rous Ray,
And op'd those Eyes that must eclipse the Day;
Now Lapdogs give themselves the rowzing Shake,
And sleepless Lovers, just at Twelve, awake:

2.

The merry brown hares came leaping
    Over the crest of the hill,
Where the clover and corn lay sleeping
    Under the moonlight still.

3.

The sun shone, having no alternative, on the nothing new.

4.

    Busie old foole, unruly Sunne,
    Why dost thou thus,
Through windowes, and through curtaines call on us?
Must to thy motions lovers seasons run?

5.

Shelley's pen slipped
referring to the Sun
Isle Continent Ocean
The date July 1st 1822
across "?fury" may be
"day" or "fiery"

6.

With how sad steps, O moon, thou climb'st the skies!
   How silently, and with how wan a face!
What! may it be that even in heavenly place
   That busy archer his sharp arrows tries?

7.

When I came last to Ludlow
   Amidst the moonlight pale,
Two friends kept step beside me,
   Two honest lads and hale.

B: _____

1.

How dreary—to be—Somebody!
How public—like a Frog—
To tell one's name—the livelong June—
To an admiring Bog!

2.

I love at early morn, from new mown swath,
To see the startled frog his route pursue;

3.

    The air was thick with a bass chorus.
Right down the dam gross-bellied frogs were cocked
On sods; their loose necks pulsed like sails. Some hopped.
The slap and plop were obscene threats,

4.

No animal will more repay
    A treatment kind and fair;
At least so lonely people say
Who keep a frog (and by the way
They are extremely rare).

5.

I myself have killed a frog twelve times, and brought him to
life eleven; but the twelfth time he died. I have a phial of the
drug which killed him in my pocket, and shall not rest until I
have discovered its antidote.

6.

The mangled Frog abides incog,
The uninteresting actual frog:
The hypothetic frog alone
Is the one frog we dwell upon.

7.

'Conversation, indeed!' said the Rocket. 'You have talked the whole time yourself. That is not conversation.'

'Somebody must listen,' answered the Frog, 'and I like to do all the talking myself. It saves time, and prevents arguments.'

'But I like arguments,' said the Rocket.

'I hope not,' said the Frog complacently. 'Arguments are extremely vulgar, for everybody in good society holds exactly the same opinions.'

C: _____

1.

Poor melancholy bird — that all night long
    Tell'st to the Moon thy tale of tender woe;
    From what sad cause can such sweet sorrow flow,
And whence this mournful melody of song?

2.

Now came still Evening on, and Twilight gray
Had in her sober Liverie all things clad;
Silence accompanied her, for Beast and Bird,
They to thir grassie Couch, these to thir Nests
Were slunk, all but the wakeful Nightingale;
She all night long her amorous descant sung;

3.

'Here indeed is the true lover,' said the Nightingale. 'What I
sing of, he suffers: what is joy to me, to him is pain. Surely
Love is a wonderful thing. It is more precious than emeralds,
and dearer than fine opals. Pearls and pomegranates cannot
buy it, nor is it set forth in the market-place.'

4.

Or, where the Virgin Orb of Night
    Silvers o'er the Forest wide,
    Or across the silent tide,
Flings her soft and quiv'ring light:
    Where, beneath some aged Tree,
    Sounds of mournful Melody,
Caught from the Nightingale's enamour'd Tale,
Steal on faint Echo's ear, and float upon the gale.

5.

It was the nightingale, and not the lark,
That pierced the fearful hollow of thine ear;
Nightly she sings on yon pomegranate-tree:
Believe me, love, it was the nightingale.

6.

Make me content
With some sweetness
From Wales
Whose nightingales
Have no wings, —
From Wiltshire and Kent
And Herefordshire,
And the villages there, —
From the names, and the things
No less.

7.

What bird so sings, yet so does wail?
O 'tis the ravish'd nightingale.
Jug, jug, jug, jug, tereu! she cries,
And still her woes at midnight rise.

D: _____

1.

Like a very small child this large muscular creature would sit down beside him because she felt lonely, and because youth most rightly resents isolation, and because she had not yet learnt her hard lesson — she had not yet learnt that the loneliest place in this world is the no-man's-land of sex.

2.

Experience, already reduced to a swarm of impressions, is ringed round for each one of us by that thick wall of personality through which no real voice has ever pierced on its way to us, or from us to that which we can only conjecture to be without. Every one of these impressions is the impression of the individual in his isolation, each mind keeping as a solitary prisoner its own dream of a world.

3.

But here the Autumn melancholy dwells,
    And sighs her tearful spells
Amongst the sunless shadows of the plain.
    Alone, alone,
    Upon a mossy stone,
She sits and reckons up the dead and gone,
With the last leaves for a love-rosary;

4.

I know nothing — nothing in the world — of the hearts of men. I only know that I am alone — horribly alone. No hearthstone will ever again witness, for me, friendly intercourse. No smoking-room will ever be other than people with incalculable simulacra amidst smoke wreaths.

5.

I hoped we would meet again the next time he found himself
in London, but for now I had an engagement with someone,
to do some sightseeing.

In that case, he said, I will spend the day in solicitude.

You mean solitude, I said.

I do beg your pardon, he said. Of course, I mean solitude.

6.

Alone, alone, all, all alone,
Alone on the wide wide sea;
And Christ would take no pity on
My soul in agony.

7.

And God stepped out on space,
And he looked around and said:
I'm lonely—
I'll make me a world.

E: _____

1.

All night have the roses heard
The flute, violin, bassoon;
All night has the casement jessamine stirr'd
To the dancers dancing in tune;
Till a silence fell with the waking bird,
And a hush with the setting moon.

2.

There never was, since the days of Darius, such a brilliant train
of camp-followers as hung round the Duke of Wellington's
army in the Low Countries, in 1815; and led it dancing and
feasting, as it were, up to the very brink of battle. A certain ball
which a noble Duchess gave at Brussels on the 15th of June in
the above-named year is historical. All Brussels had been in a
state of excitement about it, and I have heard from ladies who
were in that town at the period, that the talk and interest of
persons of their own sex regarding the ball was much greater
even than in respect of the enemy in their front.

3.

Whenever I see you
at parties I just
giggle or shrug.
It seems that I know
you so much. It seems
there must be something
we can talk about. Isn't
there? We have so much
in common. I like you.

4.

Oh say can you see Alma. The darling
of Them. All her friends were artists.
They alone have memories. They alone
love flowers. They alone give parties
and die. Poor Alma. They alone.

5.

We past a most extraordinary evening. A *private* ball this was
called, so I expected to have seen about four or five couple;
but Lord! my dear Sir, I believe I saw half the world! Two very
large rooms were full of company; in one, were cards for the
elderly ladies, and in the others were the dancers. My mamma
Mirvan, for she always calls me her child, said she would sit
with Maria and me till we were provided with partners, and
then join the card-players.

6.

However, *there* he was—and dancing
   With the fair Sylph, light as a feather;
They look'd like two fresh sunbeams, glancing,
   At daybreak, down to earth together.

7.

He drove through the park very fast, and they were soon out
of sight; and nothing more of them was seen till their return,
which did not happen till after the return of all the rest. They
both seemed delighted with their drive, but said
only in general terms that they had kept in the
lanes, while the others went on the downs.
   It was settled that there should be a dance
in the evening, and that every body should be
extremely merry all day long.

JULY

A: _____

1.

The hour glass whispers to the lion's roar,
The clock-towers tell the gardens day and night
How many errors Time has patience for,
How wrong they are in always being right.

2.

My brain, methinks, is like an hour-glass,
Wherein, my imaginations run, like sands
Filling up time; but then are turned, and turned.

3.

The years like great black oxen tread the world
And God the herdsman goads them on behind,
And I am broken by their passing feet.

4.

A poem should be motionless in time
As the moon climbs,

Leaving, as the moon releases
Twig by twig the night-entangled trees,

Leaving, as the moon behind the winter leaves,
Memory by memory the mind—

5.

The calmest thoughts come round us; as of leaves
    Budding—fruit ripening in stillness—Autumn suns
Smiling at eve upon the quiet sheaves—
Sweet Sappho's cheek—a smiling infant's breath—
    The gradual sand that through an hour-glass runs—
A woodland rivulet—a Poet's death.

6.

Had we but world enough, and time,
This coyness, lady, were no crime.

7.

Meeting with Time, slack thing, said I,
Thy sithe is dull; whet it for shame.
No marvell Sir, he did replie,
If it at length deserve some blame:
    But where one man would have me grinde it,
    Twentie for one too sharp do finde it.

B: _____

1.

"How does one mend one's way? I suppose one joins the League of Nations Union, and then reads the Isis every week, and drinks coffee in the morning at the Cadena café, and smokes a great pipe and plays hockey and goes out to tea on Boar's Hill and to lectures at Keble, and rides a bicycle with a little tray full of notebooks, and drinks cocoa in the evening and discusses sex seriously."

2.

Much have ye suffered from Time's gnawing tooth:
Yet, O ye spires of Oxford! domes and towers!
Gardens and groves! your presence overpowers
The soberness of reason; till, in sooth,
Transformed and rushing on a bold exchange
I slight my own beloved Cam

3.

The fellows of my time were decent easy men, who supinely enjoyed the gifts of the founder; their days were filled by a series of uniform employments; the chapel and the hall, the coffee house and the common room: From the toll of reading, or thinking, or writing, they had absolved their conscience.

4.

'There's something about this place,' said Peter presently, 'that alters all one's values.' He paused, and added a little abruptly: 'I have said a good deal to you one way and another, lately; but you may have noticed that since we came to Oxford I have not asked you to marry me.'

5.

How could the wind be so strong, so far inland, that cyclists coming into town in the late afternoon looked more like sailors in peril? This was on the way into Cambridge, up Mill Road past the cemetery and the workhouse.

6.

He used to write to me at one time. Long letters about Ford Madox Ford. I used to write to him, too, come to think of it. Long letters about... oh, W. B. Yeats, I suppose. That was the time we were both editors of poetry magazines. Him at Cambridge, me at Oxford.

7.

I was not train'd in Academic bowers,
And to those learned streams I nothing owe
Which copious from those twin fair founts do flow;
Mine have been any thing but studious hours.
Yet can I fancy, wandering 'mid thy towers,
Myself a nursling, Granta, of thy lap;
My brow seems tightening with the Doctor's cap,
And I walk *gowned*; feel unusual powers.

C: _____

I.

The sky and sea are parting like an oyster shell, with a low red gape. Looking across from the veranda at it, one shivers. Not that it is cold. The morning is not at all cold. But the ominousness of it: that long red slit between a dark sky and a dark Ionian sea, terrible old bivalve which has held life between its lips so long. And here, at this house, we are ledged so awfully above the dawn, naked to it.

2.

They went to the sands, to watch the flowing of the tide, which a fine south-easterly breeze was bringing in with all the grandeur which so flat a shore admitted. They praised the morning; gloried in the sea; sympathized in the delight of the fresh-feeling breeze—and were silent; till Henrietta suddenly began again, with,

'Oh! yes,—I am quite convinced that, with very few exceptions, the sea-air always does good.'

3.

'Now, am I not kind to bring you here? And look.' She led him to the side of the rampart, where a line of flat stones inserted sideways into the wall served as rough steps down to a lower walk. 'These are the very steps that Jane Austen made Louisa Musgrove fall down in *Persuasion*.'

'How romantic.'

'Gentlemen were romantic ... then.'

4·

Under the flimsiest of pretexts (this was our very last chance, and nothing really mattered) we escaped from the café to the beach, and found a desolate stretch of sand, and there, in the violet shadow of some red rocks forming a kind of cave, had a brief session of avid caresses, with somebody's lost pair of sunglasses for only witness.

5·

The day her mother died, my mother
was on holiday. I travelled to the seaside
with bad news. She slumped over the table,
spilling wine across the telegram.

6.

The marine tendency of George IV was inherited by his brother William IV, who was known as the Sailor King on account of his readiness to create any number of piers at moments of political crisis.

7·

There on the sand not far from the lovers lay the old sheep's skull without its jaw. Clean, white, wind-swept, sand-rubbed, a more unpolluted piece of bone existed nowhere on the coast of Cornwall. The sea holly would grow through the eye-sockets; it would turn to powder, or some golfer, hitting his ball one fine day, would disperse a little dust.

D: _____

1.

Sometimes I have loved the peacefulness of an ordinary
Sunday. It is like standing in a newly planted garden after
a warm rain. You can feel the silent and invisible life. All it
needs from you is that you take care not to trample on it.
And that was such a quiet day, rain on the roof, rain against
the windows, and everyone grateful, since it seems we never
do have quite enough rain.

2.

When a day that you happen to know is Wednesday starts off
by sounding like Sunday, there is something seriously wrong
somewhere.
  I felt that from the moment I woke. And yet, when I started
functioning a little more smartly, I became doubtful.

3.

Having silenced Objection by force of unreason, Will walked
to Lowick as if he had been on the way to Paradise, crossing
Halsell Common and skirting the wood, where the sunlight
fell broadly under the budding boughs, bringing out the
beauties of moss and lichen, and fresh green growths piercing
the brown. Everything seemed to know that it was Sunday,
and to approve of his going to Lowick Church.

4.

Once, early in the morning,
    Beelzebub arose,
With care his sweet person adorning,
    He put on his Sunday clothes.

5.

He battled with Shakespeare all one Sunday afternoon, and found the 'English Literature,' with which Mr. Woodrow had equipped him, had vanished down some crack in his mind. He had no doubt it was very splendid stuff, but he couldn't quite make out what it was all about. There was an occult meaning, he knew, in literature, and he had forgotten it.

6.

A year elapsed before this Clerk began
To treat the rustic something like a man;
He then in trifling points the youth advised,
Talk'd of his coat, and had it modernised;
Or with the lad a Sunday-walk would take,
And kindly strive his passions to awake;

7.

It is Sunday evening. Sometimes I feel I'd like to write a whole book of short stories and call each one Sunday. Women are far more 'sensitive' to Sundays than to the moon or their monthly period — Does Sunday mean to you something vivid and strange and remembered with longing —

E: _____

1.

By natural deformity, or accidental distortion, his vital functions were so much disordered, that his life was a *long disease*. His most frequent assailant was the headach, which he used to relieve by inhaling the steam of coffee.

2.

What thoughts I have of you tonight, Walt Whitman, for I walked down the sidestreets under the trees with a headache self-conscious looking at the full moon.

In my hungry fatigue, and shopping for images, I went into the neon fruit supermarket, dreaming of your enumerations!

3.

So I took a sheet of cardboard from the desk, wrote CLOSED UNTIL FURTHER NOTICE on it in as tidy a set of capitals as I could manage, and propped it in the window. Then I turned off the lights and made my way home.

I'd hoped the weather might be breaking at last, but the sky was blank and bright and my head immediately began to ache.

4.

       Get very drunk, and when
You wake with headache, you shall see what then.

5.

When you're lying awake with a dismal headache, and
    repose is taboo'd by anxiety,
I conceive you may use any language you choose to indulge
    in, without impropriety;
For your brain is on fire — the bed-clothes conspire of usual
    slumber to plunder you;
First your counterpane goes, and uncovers your toes, and
    your sheet slips demurely from under you;

6.

There is the blonde who gives you the up-from-under look
and smells lovely and shimmers and hangs on your arm and
is always very tired when you take her home. She makes that
helpless gesture and has that goddamned headache and you
would like to slug her except that you are glad you found out
about the headache before you invested too much time and
money and hope in her. Because the headache will always be
there, a weapon that never wears out and is as deadly as the
bravo's rapier or Lucrezia's poison vial.

7.

And in truth the much-prized wine of Auxerre has itself but
a fugitive charm, being apt to sicken and turn gross long
before the bottle is empty, however carefully sealed; as it goes,
indeed, at its best, by hard names, among those who grow it,
such as *Chainette* and *Migraine*.

AUGUST

A: _____

I.

August for the people and their favourite islands.
Daily the steamers sidle up to meet
The effusive welcome of the pier, and soon
The luxuriant life of the steep stone valleys,
The sallow oval faces of the city
Begot in passion or good-natured habit,
Are caught by waiting coaches, or laid bare
Beside the undiscriminating sea.

2.

As soon as he'd left the pavements for the soft, paper-littered sand he knew he was where he didn't want to be. Nothing for him here but this wide stretch of fine dust, this shallow sea ten minutes' march away and people in deck chairs, on rugs, behind gaudy wind-breaks, lying stripped and red, oiled in the sunshine. He'd take his shoes off, roll his trousers and paddle ludicrously as his father had done twenty years ago.

3.

Nothing of special moment to the interests of our story occurred during those six weeks, unless the proceedings of the young married couple by the sea-side may be thought to have any special interest. With regard to those proceedings I can only say that Crosbie was very glad when they were brought to a close. All holiday-making is hard work, but holiday-making with nothing to do is the hardest work of all.

4.

Proceed great days! till learning fly the shore,
Till birch shall blush with noble blood no more,
Till Thames see Eton's sons for ever play,
Till Westminster's whole year be holiday;
Till Isis' elders reel, their pupils sport;
And Alma Mater lye dissolv'd in port!

5.

When we arrived yesterday, the four of us, I shouted loudly
in the street so as not to sound nervous. I wasn't confident
about all the luggage we had brought, because it looked as if
we had come for a month, rather than a night and a day and a
morning. Victorian Norman had his haversack, because he's
going straight up north afterwards and will camp on the way,

6.

Thus it came about that, three days later, I descended from
the train at Styles St. Mary, an absurd little station, with no
apparent reason for existence, perched up in the midst of
green fields and country lanes. John Cavendish was waiting
on the platform, and piloted me out to the car.

'Got a drop of petrol still, you see,' he remarked. 'Mainly
owing to the mater's activities.'

7.

Gaffers, gammers, huzzies, louts,
    Couples, gangs, and families
Sprawling, shake, with Babel-shouts
    Bluff King Hal's funereal trees;
And eddying groups of stare-abouts
    Quiz the sandstone Hercules.

B: _____

1.

The swimming pool in the grounds of the tourist villa was more like a pond than the languid blue pools in holiday brochures. A pond in the shape of a rectangle, carved from stone by a family of Italian stonecutters living in Antibes. The body was floating near the deep end, where a line of pine trees kept the water cool in their shade.

2.

At Shanklin one has to adopt the detestable custom of bathing in drawers. If ladies don't like to see men naked why don't they keep away from the sight? To-day I had a pair of drawers given me which I could not keep on. The rough waves stripped them off and tore them down round my ancles. While thus fettered I was seized and flung down by a heavy sea which retreating suddenly left me lying naked on the sharp shingle from which I rose streaming with blood.

3.

And as some *Creatures* by their *shapes* do flye,
Some *swim*, some *run*, some *creep*, some *riseth high*.
So *Planets* by their *shapes* about do wind,
All being made, like *Circles*, round we find.

4.

The very first morning they took a leaping-pole with them, a slender ash sapling, rather more than twice their own height, which they picked out from a number in the rick-yard, intending to jump to and fro the brook on the way. But before they had got half way to the brook they altered their minds, becoming eager for the water, and raced to the bathing-place. The pole was now to be an oar, and they were to swim, supported by an oar, like shipwrecked people.

5.

We went down to the beach. The sun was still high, but a fresh wind had risen, and the sea didn't look particularly inviting; I was recovering, as it happened, from a bad cold, and decided not to bathe myself.

Gerald, already half-undressed, gave me a mocking grin.

'Not coming in, eh? All right, I won't try and force you. ...' He paused, then added, with a slight chuckle: 'You never would bathe when I asked you to, would you?'

6.

I wasn't capable of swimming round as far as your rudder-chains. And, lo and behold! there was a ladder to get hold of. After I gripped it I said to myself, 'What's the good?' When I saw a man's head looking over I thought I would swim away presently and leave him shouting — in whatever language it was. I didn't mind being looked at. I — I liked it. And then you speaking to me so quietly   as if you had expected me — made me hold on a little longer. It had been a confounded lonely time — I don't mean while swimming. I was glad to talk a little to somebody that didn't belong to the *Sephora*.

7.

Dabbling on shore half-naked sea-boys crowd,
Swim round a ship, or swing upon the shroud;
Or in a boat purloin'd, with paddles play,
And grow familiar with the watery way.

C: _____

1.

That a King-fisher hanged by the bill, sheweth in what quarter
the wind is by an occult and secret propriety, converting the
breast to that point of the Horizon from whence the wind
doth blow, is a received opinion, and very strange.

2.

But not these things are the factors. Not the birds.
The legends are
legends. Dead, hung up indoors, the kingfisher
will not indicate a favoring wind,
or avert the thunderbolt. Nor, by its nesting,
still the waters, with the new year, for seven days.
It is true, it does nest with the opening year, but not
    on the waters.

3.

And thus methinks should men of judgement frame
Their means of traffic from the vulgar trade,
And as their wealth increaseth, so enclose
Infinite riches in a little room.
But now, how stands the wind?
Into what corner peers my halcyon's bill?
Ha, to the east? Yes. See how stands the vanes?
East and by south:

4.

The step was light as thistledown. If Adam had not had the rush of the running water in his ears too loudly for him to be able to hear any other noise, he might have thought this delicate, hesitant step was the beating of his own blood.

But, suddenly, something like a kingfisher streaked across the kitchen in a glimmer of green skirts and flying gold hair, and the chime of a laugh was followed a second later by the slam of the gate leading through the starveling garden out on to the Downs.

5.

As kingfishers catch fire, dragonflies draw flame;
As tumbled over rim in roundy wells
Stones ring; like each tucked string tells, each hung bell's
Bow swung finds tongue to fling out broad its name;
Each mortal thing does one thing and the same:

6.

　　　After the kingfisher's wing
Has answered light to light, and is silent, the light is still
At the still point of the turning world.

7.

O! let me haunt this peaceful shade;
Nor let ambition e'er invade
The tenants of this leafy bow'r,
That shun her paths, and slight her pow'r.

Hither the plaintive halcyon flies
From social meads and open skies;
Pleas'd, by this rill, her course to steer,
And hide her sapphire plumage here.

D: _____

1.

For a minute or two she stood looking at the house, and wondering what to do next, when suddenly a footman in livery came running out of the wood—(she considered him to be a footman because he was in livery: otherwise, judging by his face only, she would have called him a fish)—and rapped loudly at the door with his knuckles.

2.

Knock, knock; never at quiet! What are you? But this place is too cold for hell. I'll devil-porter it no further: I had thought to have let in some of all professions that go the primrose way to the everlasting bonfire.

3.

The door between me and there was half open. I listened and decided that somebody had just looked in at the wrong office and left without entering. Then there was a small knocking on wood. Then the kind of cough you use for the same purpose. I got my feet off the desk, stood up and looked out. There she was. And nobody ever looked less like Lady Macbeth.

4.

So how many gates I swing open? How many houses I knock on? Let me count the doors that opened slow and shut quick without even me breath managing to get inside. Man, these English landlords and ladies could come up with excuses. If I had still been in uniform — a Brylcreem boy in blue — would they have seen me different?

5.

What is the knocking?
What is the knocking at the door in the night?
It is somebody wants to do us harm.

No, no, it is the three strange angels.
Admit them, admit them

6.

When you stop to tattle with some crony Servant in the
same Street, leave your own Street-Door open, that you may
get in without knocking, when you come back; otherwise
your Mistress may know you are gone out, and you may be
chidden.

7.

His words were interrupted by a sharp rat-tat from the
direction of the inner door.
    'What the deuce is he knocking at his own door for?' cried
the clerk.
    Again and much louder came the rat-tat-tat. We all gazed
expectantly at the closed door. Glancing at H—, I saw his face
turn rigid, and he leaned forward in intense excitement. Then
suddenly came a low guggling, gargling sound and a brisk
drumming upon woodwork.

E: _____

1.

Now air is hushed, save where the weak-ey'd bat
With short shrill shriek flits by on leathern wing,
    Or where the beetle winds
    His small but sullen horn
As oft he rises 'midst the twilight path
Against the pilgrim, borne in heedless hum:

2.

The face of the heath by its mere complexion added half an
hour to evening; it could in like manner retard the dawn,
sadden noon, anticipate the frowning of storms scarcely
generated, and intensify the opacity of a moonless midnight
to a cause of shaking and dread.

3.

Little girl, it is time to retire to your rest,
    The sheep are put into the fold,
The linnet forsakes us and flies to her nest,
    To shelter her young from the cold.

4.

It is the evening of this unrestful day of rest and the far barn
that has survived the fire is full of harvesters, lying back on
bales of hay and building up an appetite on rich man's yellow
manchet bread

5.

The light passes
from ridge to ridge,
from flower to flower —
the hypaticas wide-spread
under the light
grow faint

6.

The sun drops luridly into the west;
Darkness has raised her arms to draw him down
Before the time, not waiting as of wont
Till he has come to her behind the sea;
And the smooth waves grow sullen in the gloom

7.

Even is come; and from the dark Park, hark,
The signal of the setting sun — one gun!
And six is sounding from the chime, prime time
To go and see the Drury-Lane Dane slain —
Or hear Othello's jealous doubt spout out,

SEPTEMBER

A: _____

1.

The city now doth, like a garment, wear
The beauty of the morning; silent, bare,
Ships, towers, domes, theatres, and temples lie
Open unto the fields, and to the sky;

2.

God made the country, and man made the town.
What wonder then, that health and virtue, gifts
That can alone make sweet the bitter draught
That life holds out to all, should most abound
And least be threatened in the fields and groves?

3.

Long ago, in 1945, all the nice people in England were poor,
allowing for exceptions. The streets of the cities were lined
with buildings in bad repair or in no repair at all, bomb-sites
piled with stony rubble, houses like giant teeth in which decay
had been drilled out, leaving only the cavity.

4.

And wee will sit upon the Rocks,
Seeing the Sheepheards feed theyr flocks,
By shallow Rivers, to whose falls,
Melodious byrds sing Madrigalls.

5.

I'll handle dainties on the docks
And thou shalt read of summer frocks:
At evening by the sour canals
We'll hope to hear some madrigals.

6.

... and then the building of more, strongly, beautifully, and in groups of limited extent, kept in proportion to their streams, and walled round, so that there may be no festering and wretched suburb anywhere, but clean and busy street within, and the open country without, with a belt of beautiful garden and orchard round the walls, so that from any part of the city perfectly fresh air and grass, and sight of far horizon, might be reachable in a few minutes' walk.

7.

In London, the rich disdain the poor. The courtier the citizen. The citizen the countryman. One occupation disdaineth another. The merchant the retailer. The retailer the craftsman. The better sort of craftsmen the baser. The shoemaker the cobbler. The cobbler the carman.

B: _____

1.

Last night in Notting Hill
I saw Blake passing by
Who saw Ezekiel
Airborne in Peckham Rye

2.

Somewhere afield here something lies
In Earth's oblivious eyeless trust
That moved a poet to prophecies –
A pinch of unseen, unguarded dust:

The dust of the lark that Shelley heard,
And made immortal through times to be;

3.

John Keats, who was kill'd off by one critique,
    Just as he really promised something great,
If not intelligible, without Greek
    Contrived to talk about the gods of late,
Much as they might have been supposed to speak.
    Poor fellow! His was an untoward fate: –
'Tis strange the mind, that very fiery particle,
    Should let itself be snuffed out by an Article.

4.

To draw no envy, Shakespeare, on thy name,
Am I thus ample to thy book and fame;
While I confess thy writings to be such
As neither man nor muse can praise too much;

5.

Next with a gentle Dart strike *Dryden* down,
Who but begins to aim at the Renown
Bestow'd on *Satyrists*, and quits the Stage,
To lash the witty Follies of the Age.

6.

His Intellectuals are very good yet (1680) and he makes verses,
but he growes feeble. He wrote verses of the Bermudas 50
yeares since, upon the information of one who had been
there; walking in his fine woods the poetique spirit came
upon him.

7.

Yet malice never was his aim;
He lash'd the vice, but spar'd the name;
No individual could resent,
Where thousands equally were meant.
His satire points at no defect,
But what all mortals may correct;

C: _____

1.

"What I tell you three times is true."

2.

Generations have trod, have trod, have trod;

3.

Never, never, never, never, never.

4.

and yes I said yes I will Yes

5.

She, she, she, and only she

6.

Cottleston, Cottleston, Cottleston Pie,
A fish can't whistle and neither can I.

7.

Sweet sweet sweet sweet sweet tea.

D: _____

1.

"Why do you sit, O pale thin man,
　　At the end of the room
By that harpsichord, built on the quaint old plan?
　　—It is cold as a tomb,
And there's not a spark within the grate;
　　And the jingling wires
　　Are as vain desires
　　That have lagged too late."

2.

　　　　And what if all of animated nature
Be but organic Harps diversely fram'd,
That tremble into thought, as o'er them sweeps
Plastic and vast, one intellectual breeze,
At once the Soul of each, and God of all?

3.

When I play on my fiddle in Dooney,
Folk dance like a wave of the sea;
My cousin is priest in Kilvarnet,
My brother in Moharabuiee.

4.

When the Day that he must go hence, was come, many
accompanied him to the River side, into which as he went, he
said, *Death, where is thy Sting?* — And as he went down deeper,
he said, *Grave, where is thy Victory?* — So he passed over, and all
the Trumpets sounded for him on the other side.

5.

With my 'Pilly-willy-pinky-winky-popp!'
   (Oh, it's any tune that comes into my head!)
So I keep 'em moving forward till they drop;
   So I play 'em up to water and to bed.

6.

There was a barrel-organ playing at the corner of Torrington
Square. It played *Destiny* and *La Paloma* and *Le Rêve Passe*, all
tunes I liked, and the wind was warm and kind not spiteful,
which doesn't often happen in London.

7.

My lute awake! Perform the last
Labour that thou and I shall waste,
And end that I have now begun;
For when this song is sung and past,
My lute, be still for I have done

E: _____

1.

She was only four foot ten. I made love to her in the sweetness of the weary morning. Then, two tired angels of some kind, hung-up forlornly in an LA shelf, having found the closest and most delicious thing in life together, we fell asleep and slept till late afternoon.

2.

I grant the linnet, lark and bull-finch sing,
But best the dear good angel of the Spring,

3.

There had been a grave debate in the servants' hall about the exact status of angels. Even Mr. Blenkinsop, the butler, had been uncertain. 'Angels are certainly not guests,' he had said, 'and I don't think they are deputations. Nor they ain't governesses, nor clergy, not strictly speaking; they're not entertainers, because entertainers *dine* nowadays, the more's the pity.'

4.

At thy Nativity a glorious Quire
Of Angels in the fields of *Bethlehem* sung
To Shepherds watching at their folds by night,
And told them the Messiah now was born,
Where they might see him, and to thee they came,
Directed to the Manger where thou lais't,

5.

Our job is to arrange for the arrival
of angels, by the coachload, in white vests.

6.

First we lov'd well and faithfully,
Yet knew not what wee lov'd, nor why,
Difference of sex no more wee knew,
Than our Guardian Angells doe;

7.

How angel-like he sings!

OCTOBER

A: _____

1.

'Cat!' repeated the old gentleman. 'Puss, Kit, Tit, Grimalkin, Tabby, Brindle! Whoosh!' with which last sound, uttered in a hissing manner between his teeth, the old gentleman swung his arms violently round and round.

2.

Her conscious tail her joy declared;
The fair round face, the snowy beard,
   The velvet of her paws,
Her coat that with the tortoise vies,
Her ears of jet and emerald eyes,
   She saw; and purred applause.

3.

I shall never forget the indulgence with which he treated Hodge, his cat; for whom he himself used to go out and buy oysters, lest the servants, having that trouble, should take a dislike to the poor creature.

4.

For I will consider my Cat Jeoffry.
For he is the servant of the Living God duly and daily serving
   him.
For at the first glance of the glory of God in the East he
   worships in his way.
For is this done by wreathing his body seven times round
   with elegant quickness.
For then he leaps up to catch the musk, which is the blessing
   of God upon his prayer.
For he rolls upon prank to work it in.

5.

He bent down to her, his hands on his knees.

—Milk for the pussens, he said.

—Mrkgnao! the cat cried.

They call them stupid. They understand what we say better than we understand them. She understands all she wants to. Vindictive too. Wonder what I look like to her.

6.

Eppie, with the rippling radiance of her hair and the whiteness of her rounded chin and throat set off by the dark-blue cotton gown, laughing merrily as the kitten held on with her four claws to one shoulder, like a design for a jughandle, while Snap on the right hand and Puss on the other put up their paws towards a morsel which she held out of the reach of both – Snap occasionally desisting in order to remonstrate with the cat by a cogent worrying growl on the greediness and futility of her conduct; till Eppie relented, caressed them both, and divided the morsel between them.

7.

Yet some great souls on gain so keen are set,
They'll *eat a cat* to win a trifling bett!
While some, in worsted hose and shabby *scratch*,
Ride fifty miles to see — a *boxing match* !
Though *few*,— but to obtain some secret end,
Would cross the threshold to *relieve a friend* !

B: _____

1.

Herbs, garlic,
cheese, please let me in!
Souffles, salads,
Parker House rolls,
please let me in!
Cook Helen,
why are you so cross,
why is your kitchen verboten?

2.

One of those chaps would make short work of a fellow. Pick
the bones clean no matter who it was. Ordinary meat for
them. A corpse is meat gone bad. Well and what's cheese?

3.

'Hellish dark and smells of cheese.'

4.

'Many's the long night I've dreamed of cheese — toasted,
mostly.'

5.

        I had rather live
With cheese and garlic in a windmill, far,
Than feed on cates and have him talk to me
In any summer-house in Christendom.

6.

Place toast and cheese in the middle of the dressed plates and serve. A simple dish but one with pleasant contrasts of heat and coolness, the freshness of the salad and the gamey warmth of its proteinous counterpart.

Cheese is philosophically interesting as a food whose qualities depend on the action of bacteria — it is, as James Joyce remarked, 'the corpse of milk'.

7.

... the circumjacent region of sitting-room was of a comparatively pastureless and shifty character: imposing on the waiter the wandering habits of putting the covers on the floor (where he fell over them), the melted butter in the armchair, the bread on the bookshelves, the cheese in the coalscuttle, and the boiled fowl into my bed in the next room – where I found much of its parsley and butter in a state of congelation when I retired for the night.

C: _____

1.

At the top of the house the apples are laid in rows,
And the skylight lets the moonlight in, and those
Apples are deep-sea apples of green. There goes
A cloud on the moon in the autumn night.

2.

To satisfie the sharp desire I had
Of tasting those fair Apples, I resolv'd
Not to deferr; hunger and thirst at once,
Powerful perswaders, quick'nd at the scent
Of that alluring fruit, urg'd me so keene.

3.

'The world must exist, to have the shape of a pear; and that the
world is shaped like a pear, and not like an apple, as the fools
of Oxford say, I have satisfactorily proved in my book. Now, if
there were no world, what would become of my system? But
what do you propose to do in London?'

4.

Whann the fayre apple, rudde as even skie,
Do bende the tree unto the fructyle grounde;
When joicie peres, and berries of blacke die,
Doe daunce in ayre, and call the eyne arounde ...

5.

I will find out where she has gone,
And kiss her lips and take her hands;
And walk among long dappled grass,
And pluck till time and times are done
The silver apples of the moon,
The golden apples of the sun.

6.

One good gift has the fatal apple given, —
Your reason: — let it not be overswayed
By tyrannous threats to force you into faith
'Gainst all external sense and inward feeling:
Think and endure, — and form an inner world
In your own bosom — where the outward fails;
So shall you nearer be the spiritual
Nature, and war triumphant with your own.

7.

Lo! sweeten'd with the summer light,
The full-juic'd apple, waxing over-mellow,
Drops in a silent autumn night.

D: _____

1.

And now, each night I count the stars,
And each night I get the same number.
And when they will not come to be counted,
I count the holes they leave.

2.

The sun descending in the west,
The evening star does shine;
The birds are silent in their nest,
And I must seek for mine.

3.

Bright spark, shot from a brighter place,
   Where beams surround my Saviour's face,
      Canst thou be any where
         So well as there?

4.

On a starred night Prince Lucifer uprose.
Tired of his dark dominion swung the fiend
Above the rolling ball in cloud part screened,
Where sinners hugged their spectre of repose.

5.

There was music from my neighbor's house through the
summer nights. In his blue gardens men and girls came and
went like moths among the whisperings and the champagne
and the stars.

6.

There, by the starlit fences,
  The wanderer halts and hears
My soul that lingers sighing
  About the glimmering weirs.

7.

Oh, float into our azure heaven again!
Be there Love's folding-star at thy return;
The living Sun will feed thee from its urn
Of golden fire; the Moon will veil her horn
In thy last smiles; adoring Even and Morn
Will worship thee with incense of calm breath
And lights and shadows;

E: _____

1.

Life is first boredom, then fear.

2.

Mr. James Harthouse passed a whole night and a day in a state of so much hurry, that the World, with its best glass in his eye, would scarcely have recognized him during that insane interval, as the brother Jem of the honourable and jocular member. He was positively agitated. He several times spoke with an emphasis, similar to the vulgar manner. He went in and went out in an unaccountable way, like a man without an object. He rode like a highwayman. In a word, he was so horribly bored by existing circumstances, that he forgot to go in for boredom in the manner prescribed by the authorities.

3.

"... the only way a woman can ever reform a man is by boring him so completely that he loses all possible interest in life. If you had married this girl you would have been wretched. Of course you would have treated her kindly. One can always be kind to people about whom one cares nothing."

4.

Agathocles' pot, — a Mordecai in your gate, — a Lazarus at your door, — a lion in your path, — a frog in your chamber, — a fly in your ointment, — a mote in your eye, a triumph to your enemy — an apology to your friends, — the one thing not needful, — the hail in harvest, — the ounce of sour in a pound of sweet — the bore *par excellence*.

5.

Society is now one polish'd horde
Form'd of two mighty tribes, the Bores and Bored.

6.

'I don't know. We women can't go in search of adventures —
to find out the North-West Passage or the source of the Nile,
or to hunt tigers in the East. We must stay where we grow,
or where the gardeners like to transplant us. We are brought
up like the flowers, to look as pretty as we can, and be dull
without complaining. That is my notion about the plants:
they are often bored, and that is the reason why some of them
have got poisonous.'

7.

She found Mira lolling beneath a capacious lampshade
looking inexpressibly bored. Her hostess gathered by her
silhouette that the temptation to poke a finger through a
Chinese vellum-screen, painted with water-lilies and fantastic
swooping birds, was almost more than she could endure.

'My dear, won't you dance for us?' she asked.

NOVEMBER

A: _____

1.

The Owl looked up to the stars above,
 And sang to a small guitar,
'O lovely Pussy! O Pussy, my love,
 What a beautiful Pussy you are,
  You are,
   You are!
What a beautiful Pussy you are!'

2.

At eight o'clock, I opened the window to the woods
and an owl about the size of a vicar
tumbled across in a boned gown

3.

White owls seem not (but in this I am not positive) to hoot at
all: all that clamorous hooting appears to me to come from
the wood kinds. The white owl does indeed snore and hiss
in a tremendous manner; and these menaces well answer the
intention of intimidating: for I have known a whole village up
in arms on such an occasion, imagining the church-yard to be
full of goblins and spectres.

4.

Make not your rosary of yew-berries,
 Nor let the beetle, nor the death-moth be
  Your mournful Psyche, nor the downy owl
A partner in your sorrow's mysteries;

5.

'Man,' says the Professor elsewhere, in quite antipodal contrast with these high-soaring delineations, which we have here cut short on the verge of the inane, 'man is by birth somewhat of an owl. Perhaps too of all the owleries that ever possessed him, the most owlish, if we consider it, is that of your actually existing Motive-Millwrights. Fantastic tricks enough man has played, in his time; has fancied himself to be most things, down even to an animated heap of Glass: but to fancy himself a dead Iron-Balance for weighing Pains and Pleasures on, was reserved for this his latter era.'

6.

Assiduous, in his bower, the wailing owl
Plies his sad song. The cormorant on high
Wheels from the deep, and screams along the land.
Loud shrieks the soaring hern; and with wild wing
The circling seafowl cleave the flaky clouds.

7.

Beneath yon ruin'd abbey's moss-grown piles
Oft let me sit, at twilight hour of eve,
Where through some western window the pale moon
Pours her long levelled rule of streaming light;
While sullen sacred silence reigns around,
Save the lone screech-owl's note, who builds his bow'r
Amid the mould'ring caverns dark and damp,

B: _____

1.

At this unexpectedly repressing manner in her lover the girl seemed to repress herself also. 'Of course you have seen my fire,' she answered with languid calmness, artificially maintained. 'Why shouldn't I have a bonfire on the fifth of November, like other denizens of the heath?'

'I knew it was meant for me.'

2.

The paper was heaped over this foundation of sticks and then we built up a mountain of branches dragged from the fields and the edges of the woods. When darkness came and the stars were out we lighted the vast pile, and shouted and sang as the blaze swept upwards towards the sky. Faces in the glow had a strange look, as if we were all savages, dancing round a cannibal feast.

3.

Stave-machines, planing-machines, reaping-machines,
   ploughing-machines, thrashing-machines,
   steam wagons,
The cart of the carman, the omnibus, the ponderous dray,
Pyrotechny, letting off color'd fireworks at night, fancy
   figures and jets;

4.

It was the Fifth of November, and at every turn she had met groups of children bearing their dummy towards the bonfire, on a chair or in a handcart, and assailing her with, 'Penny for the Guy.' It was curiously shocking to be confronted with these effigies, stuffed with straw, bedizened in human rags, sagging forward over the string that fastened them from the waist to their conveyance.

5.

In fireworks give him leave to vent his spite,
Those are the only serpents he can write;
The height of his ambition is, we know,
But to be master of a puppet-show;

6.

"You'd have guessed if you'd been up in the window with
me—only Dinah was making you tidy, so you couldn't. I was
watching the boys getting in sticks for the bonfire—and it
wants plenty of sticks, Kitty! Only it got so cold, and it snowed
so, they had to leave off. Never mind, Kitty, we'll go and see
the bonfire to-morrow."

7.

Go on, Madame! Go on – be bright and busy
While hoax'd Astronomers look up and stare
From tall observatories, dumb and dizzy,
To see a Squib in Cassiopeia's Chair!
A Serpent wriggling into Charles's Wain!
A Roman Candle lighting the Great Bear!
A Rocket tangled in Diana's train,
And Crackers stuck in Berenice's Hair!

C: _____

1.

By now, the first customers were emerging from the elevators, hesitating a moment with the bewildered, somewhat startled expressions that people always had on finding themselves in the toy department, then starting off on weaving courses.

'Do you have the dolls that wet?' a woman asked her.

2.

'You are coming down to us at Easter, and you always bring the boys some toys, so that will be an excellent opportunity for you to inaugurate the new experiment. Go about in the shops and buy any little toys or models that have special bearing on civilian life in its more peaceful aspects.'

3.

Come buy, come buy:
Our grapes fresh from the vine,
Pomegranates full and fine,
Dates and sharp bullaces,
Rare pears and greengages,
Damsons and bilberries,
Taste them and try.

4.

I had made a Prize of a Piece of very good Damask in a *Mercers* Shop, and went clear off myself; but had convey'd the Peice to this Companion of mine, when we went out of the Shop; and she went one way, and I went another: We had not been long out of the Shop, but the *Mercer* mist his Peice of Stuff, and sent his Messengers, one, one way, and one another, and they presently seiz'd her...

5.

Spending beyond their income on gifts for Christmas —
Swing doors and crowded lifts and draperied jungles —
What shall we buy for our husbands and sons
    Different from last year?

6.

'Now, if you are well up in your London, you will know that
the office of the company is in Fresno Street, which branches
out of Upper Swandam Lane, 13 where you found me tonight.
Mrs St Clair had her lunch, started for the City, did some
shopping, proceeded to the company's office, got her packet,
and found herself exactly at 4.35 walking through Swandam
Lane on her way back to the station. Have you followed me
so far?'

7.

And by-and-by Mary began to part with other superfluities at
the pawn-shop. The smart tea-tray, and tea-caddy, long and
carefully kept, went for bread for her father. He did not ask
for it, or complain, but she saw hunger in his shrunk, fierce,
animal look. Then the blankets went, for it was summer time,
and they could spare them; and their sale made a fund, which
Mary fancied would last till better times came.

D: _____

1.

There the musick plays you into the bath, and the women that tend you, present you with a little floating wooden dish, like a bason; in which the lady puts a handkerchief, and a nosegay, of late the snuff box is added, and some patches; tho' the bath occasioning a little perspiration, the patches do not stick as kindly as they should.

2.

Trembling, as Father Adam stood
To pull the stalk, before the Fall,
So I stand here, before the Flood,
On my own head the shock to call.

3.

It was a very hot summer, in August, 1904; and Florence had been taking the baths for a month. I don't know how it feels to be a patient at one of those places. I never was a patient anywhere. I dare say the patients get a home feeling and some sort of anchorage in the spot. They seem to like the bath attendants, with their cheerful faces, their air of authority, their white linen.

4.

As a bathtub lined with white porcelain,
When the hot water gives out or goes tepid,
So is the slow cooling of our chivalrous passion,
O my much praised but-not-altogether-satisfactory lady.

5.

She lay in the bath with the water touching
her all over, and remembered that not even
the most tender lover could do that. She wondered
if every molecule on the surface of her skin
was wet and what wet meant to such very
tiny matter.

6.

Bath ready—could scarcely bear it so hot. I persevered, and got in; very hot, but very acceptable. I lay still for some time.

On moving my hand above the surface of the water, I experienced the greatest fright I ever received in the whole course of my life; for imagine my horror on discovering my hand, as I thought, full of blood.

7.

She plunged on in the dark-grey tangible night. She found the side-door open, and slipped into her room unseen. As she closed the door the gong sounded, but she would take her bath all the same—she must take her bath. 'But I won't be late any more,' she said to herself; 'it's too annoying.'

E: _____

1.

It was *a low, dull, quick sound – much such a sound as a watch makes when enveloped in cotton.*

2.

Devouring Time, blunt thou the lion's paws,
And make the earth devour her own sweet brood;
Pluck the keen teeth from the fierce tiger's jaws,
And burn the long-liv'd Phoenix in her blood;

3.

By way of enforcing this proclamation, Mr Weller, using the watch after the manner of a president's hammer, and remarking with great pride that nothing hurt it, and that falls and concussions of all kinds materially enhanced the excellence of the works and assisted the regulator, knocked the table a great many times, and declared the association formally constituted.

4.

"That, Father! will I gladly do:
'Tis scarcely afternoon—
The minster-clock has just struck two,
And yonder is the moon!"

5.

This instrument being several years older than Oak's grandfather, had the peculiarity of going either too fast or not at all. The smaller of its hands, too, occasionally slipped round on the pivot, and thus, though the minutes were told with precision, nobody could be quite certain of the hour they belonged to.

6.

Half-way up the stairs it stands,
And points and beckons with its hands
From its case of massive oak,
Like a monk, who, under his cloak,
Crosses himself, and sighs, alas!

7.

Pray my Dear, quoth my mother, have you not forgot to
wind up the clock? — Good G..! cried my father, making
an exclamation, but taking care to moderate his voice at the
same time, — Did ever woman, since the creation of the
world, interrupt a man with such a silly question? Pray, what
was your father saying?—Nothing.

DECEMBER

A: _____

1.

　　A vision on his sleep
There came, a dream of hopes that never yet
Had flushed his cheek. He dreamed a veilèd maid
Sate near him, talking in low solemn tones.
Her voice was like the voice of his own soul
Heard in the calm of thought;

2.

I would spread the cloths under your feet:
But I, being poor, have only my dreams;
I have spread my dreams under your feet;
Tread softly because you tread on my dreams.

3.

Dear love, for nothing less than thee
Would I have broke this happy dream;
　　It was a theme
For reason, much too strong for fantasy,
Therefore thou wak'd'st me wisely; yet
My dream thou brok'st not, but continued'st it.

4.

The imagination may be compared to Adam's dream, —
he awoke and found it truth. I am more zealous in this affair
because I have never yet been able to perceive how anything
can be known for truth by consecutive reasoning — and yet
it must be.

5.

Deep into that darkness peering, long I stood there
    wondering, fearing,
Doubting, dreaming dreams no mortal ever dared to dream
    before;
But the silence was unbroken, and the darkness gave no
    token,
And the only word there spoken was the whispered word,
    "Lenore!"

6.

Ships at a distance have every man's wish on board. For some
they come in with the tide. For others they sail forever on the
horizon, never out of sight, never landing until the Watcher
turns his eyes away in resignation, his dreams mocked to
death by Time. That is the life of men.

Now, women forget those things they don't want to
remember, and remember everything they don't want to
remember. The dream is the truth.

7.

I rubbed mine Eyes often, but the same Objects still occurred.
I pinched my Arms and Sides, to awake myself, hoping I
might be in a Dream. I then absolutely concluded, that all
these Appearances could be nothing else but Necromancy
and Magick. But I had no Time to pursue these Reflections;
for the Grey Horse came to the Door, and made me a Sign to
follow him into the third Room,

B: _____

1.

Christmas is coming.
The phone rings and I curse.
Literary editor.
Seasonal verse.

Big deal. Big chance
To sell them a rhyme.
They never publish poetry
Except at Christmas-time.

2.

"You know the reason Mother proposed not having any presents this Christmas was because it is going to be a hard winter for everyone; and she thinks we ought not to spend money for pleasure, when our men are suffering so in the army. We can't do much, but we can make our little sacrifices, and ought to do it gladly. But I am afraid I don't;"

3.

So stick up *ivy* and the *bays*,
And then restore the *heathen* ways.
Green will remind you of the spring,
Though this great day denies the thing,
And mortifies the earth and all
But your wild *revels*, and loose *hall*.

4.

When the Cathedral clock struck twelve there was an answer—
like an echo of the chimes—and Simpkin heard it, and came
out of the tailor's door, and wandered about in the snow.

From all the roofs and gables and old wooden houses in
Gloucester came a thousand merry voices singing the old
Christmas rhymes—all the old songs that ever I heard of, and
some that I don't know, like Whittington's bells.

5.

When you remember that no child, until Santa Claus began
his travels, had ever known the pleasure of possessing a toy,
you will understand how joy crept into the homes of those
who had been favored with a visit from the good man, and
how they talked of him day by day in loving tones and were
honestly grateful for his kindly deeds.

6.

I am a worker, a tombstone mason, anxious to pleace avery-
buries and jully glad when Christmas comes his once ayear.
You are a poorjoist, unctuous to polise nopebobbies and
tunnibelly ooully when 'tio thime took o'er home, gin.

7.

What crowding thoughts around me wake,
What marvels in a Christmas-cake!
Ah say, what strange enchantment dwells
Enclos'd within its od'rous cells?
Is there no small magician bound
Encrusted in its snowy round?

C: _____

1.

Ring ye the bells, ye yong men of the towne,
And leave your wonted labours for this day:
This day is holy; doe ye write it downe.
That ye for ever it remember may.

2.

Your toll, O melancholy bells!
    Over the valley swells:
O touching chimes! your dying sighs
    Travel our tranquil skies.

3.

Ring out, wild bells, to the wild sky,
    The flying cloud, the frosty light:
    The year is dying in the night;
Ring out, wild bells, and let him die.

4.

Woe to any little heedless reptile of an author that ventures across their path without a safe-conduct from the Board of Controul. They snap him up at a mouthful, and sit licking their lips, stroking their whiskers, and rattling their bells over the imaginary fragments of their devoted prey, to the alarm and astonishment of the whole breed of literary, philosophical, and revolutionary vermin, that were naturalised in this country by a Prince of Orange and an Elector of Hanover a hundred years ago.

5.

The curfew tolls the knell of parting day,
The lowing herd wind slowly o'er the lea,

6.

No man is an *Iland*, intire of it selfe; every man is a peece of
the *Continent*, a part of the *maine*; if a *Clod* bee washed away by
the *Sea*, *Europe* is the lesse, as well as if a *Promontorie* were, as
well as if a *Mannor* of thy *friends* or of *thine owne* were: any mans
death diminishes *me*, because I am involved in *Mankinde*; And
therefore never send to know for whom the *bell* tolls; It tolls
for *thee*.

7.

The bells, I say, the bells break down their tower;
And swing I know not where. Their tongues engrave
Membrane through marrow, my long-scattered score
Of broken intervals …And I, their sexton slave!

D: _____

1.

O for a beaker full of the warm South,
    Full of the true, the blushful Hippocrene,
        With beaded bubbles winking at the brim,
            And purple-stained mouth;

2.

And not by eastern windows only,
    When daylight comes, comes in the light,
In front the sun climbs slow, how slowly,
    But westward, look, the land is bright.

3.

Slowly, very slowly, like two unhurried compass needles, the
feet turned towards the right; north, north-east, east, south-
east, south, south-south-west; then paused, and, after a few
seconds, turned as unhurriedly back towards the left. South-
south-west, south, south-east, east ...

4.

By the Nine Gods he swore it,
    And named a trysting day,
And bade his messengers ride forth,
East and west and south and north,
    To summon his array.

5.

The coldest winds came from the south, and the Cob House
had been built in the pathway of the winds.

6.

Running dark under their wheels the miles mounted by tens:
she felt nothing — Like a shout from the top of a bank, like
a loud chord struck on the dark, she saw: 'TO THE NORTH'
written black on white, with a long black immovably flying
arrow.

Something gave way.

7.

Oh, East is East, and West is West, and never the twain
    shall meet,
Till Earth and Sky stand presently at God's great
    Judgment Seat;

E:

1.

'Oh, to crumple this telegram in my fingers—to let the light of the world flood back—to say this has not happened! But why turn one's head hither and thither? This is the truth. This is the fact. His horse stumbled; he was thrown. The flashing trees and white rails went up in a shower. There was a surge; a drumming in his ears. Then the blow; the world crashed; he breathed heavily. He died where he fell.'

2.

The telephone rang. She lifted the receiver. As she had feared, the man spoke before she could say a word. When he had spoken the familiar sentence she said, 'Who is that speaking, who is it?'

But the voice, as on eight previous occasions, had rung off.

3.

She was dead, and past all help, or need of it. The ancient rooms she had seemed to fill with life, even while her own was waning fast—the garden she had tended—the eyes she had gladdened—the noiseless haunts of many a thoughtful hour—the paths she had trodden as it were but yesterday—could know her never more.

4.

For God's sake, let us sit upon the ground
And tell sad stories of the death of kings;
How some have been deposed; some slain in war,
Some haunted by the ghosts they have deposed;
Some poison'd by their wives: some sleeping kill'd;
All murder'd.

5.

No motion has she now, no force;
    She neither hears nor sees;
Rolled round in earth's diurnal course,
    With rocks, and stones, and trees.

6.

I have wrestled with death. It is the most unexciting contest
you can imagine. It takes place in an impalpable grayness,
with nothing underfoot, with nothing around, without
spectators, without clamour, without glory, without the great
desire of victory, without the great fear of defeat, in a sickly
atmosphere of tepid scepticism, without much belief in your
own right, and still less in that of your adversary.

7.

She dyed in her bed, suddenly. Some suspected that she was
poysoned. When her head was opened there was found but
little braine, which her husband imputed to her drinking
of viper-wine; but spitefull women would say 'twas a viper
husband who was jealous of her that she would steale a
leape.

VALEDICTORY

VALEDICTORY

1.

'The greatest part of a writer's time is spent in reading, in order
to write: a man will turn over half a library to make one book.'

2.

He reads until the chapel clock strikes five,
And gradually discovers that the book,
Unevenly, gradually, and with difficulty,
Has all along been showing him its mind
(Like no one ever met at a dinner party),
And his attention has become prolonged
To the quiet passion with which he in return
Has given himself completely to the book.

3.

All sorts read bookes, but why? will you discerne?
The foole to laugh, the wiser sort to learne.
The sight, taste, sent of cheese to some is hateful,
The sight, taste, sense of bookes to some's vngratefull.
    No cheese there was, that euer pleas'd all feeders,
    No booke there is, that euer lik't all readers.

4.

Constance trembled with painful excitement. The horror
of existence closed in upon her. She could imagine nothing
more appalling than the pass to which they had been brought
by the modern change in the lower classes.
    In the kitchen, Sophia, conscious that the moment held the
future of at least the next three weeks, collected her forces.
    'Maud,' she said, 'did you not hear me call you?'
    Maud looked up from a book—doubtless a wicked book.
    'No, ma'am.'

5.

Or, my scrofulous French novel
    On grey paper with blunt type!

Simply glance at it, you grovel
  Hand and foot in Belial's gripe;

6.

Go, litel book, go litel myn tregedie,
Ther god thy maker yet, er that he dye,
Sende might to make in som comedie!
But litel book, no making thou n'envye,
But subgit be to alle poesye;

7.

Go, little Book, from this my solitude,
  I cast thee on the waters: – go thy ways!
And if, as I believe, thy vein be good,
  The World will find thee after many days.
Be it with thee according to thy worth: –
Go, little Book! in faith I send thee forth.

8.

Go, little book, and wish to all
Flowers in the garden, meat in the hall,
A bin of wine, a spice of wit,
A house with lawns enclosing it,
A living river by the door,
A nightingale in the sycamore!

9.

So go forth to the world, to the good report and the evil!
Go, little book! thy tale, is it not evil and good?
Go, and if strangers revile, pass quietly by without answer.

10.

'If the reviewers fall idle, everybody drops dead:
it's as simple as that.

— Go, little book.'

THE
ANSWERS

NEMO'S WELCOME

1. Charles Dickens, *Great Expectations*, Ch. 1
2. John Donne, 'Aire & Angells'
3. T. S. Eliot, 'Gus, the Theatre Cat', from *Old Possum's Book of Practical Cats*
4. William Shakespeare, *Romeo and Juliet*, Act II, ii
5. Philip Larkin, 'The Old Fools'
6. Thomas De Quincey, 'On the Knocking at the Gate in Macbeth'
7. Alexander Pope, 'Elegy to the Memory of an Unfortunate Lady'
8. Daniel Defoe, *Moll Flanders*, opening sentence
9. William Blake, 'Infant Joy'
10. Jonathan Swift, *Gulliver's Travels*, Ch. 2

THE ALMANAC

*The seventh answer in each of the following 60 themed sections has been intentionally omitted to create a separate challenge: see 'How to use this book' on page xviii for more details.

JANUARY

A: WINTER

1. William Shakespeare, *Love's Labours Lost*, Act V, ii
2. Gerard Manley Hopkins, 'Ash-boughs'
3. John Donne, 'Twicknam Garden'
4. James Joyce, 'The Dead', *Dubliners*
5. Byron, *Don Juan*, Canto V, 58
6. Ann Taylor, 'Snow'
7. *

B: BREAKFAST

1. F. Scott Fitzgerald, 'May Day'
2. Thomas Love Peacock, *Crotchet Castle*, Ch. 2
3. Mark Twain, *The Adventures of Huckleberry Finn*, Ch. 8
4. Jerome K. Jerome, *Three Men in a Boat*, Ch. 11
5. Anthony Trollope, *The Warden*, Ch. VIII
6. W. S. Gilbert, *Trial By Jury* (Defendant)
7. *

C: SNOW

1. Kenneth Grahame, *The Wind in the Willows*, Ch. 3, 'The Wild Wood'
2. Robert Bridges, 'London Snow'
3. Wallace Stevens, 'The Snow Man'
4. Robert Frost, 'Stopping by Woods on a Snowy Evening'
5. Christina Rossetti, 'A Christmas Carol'
6. Jane Austen, letter to her sister, March 7, 1814
7. *

D: SKATING

1. William Wordsworth, *The Prelude*, Book I
2. Philippa Pearce, *Tom's Midnight Garden*, Ch. XXIII
3. Virginia Woolf, *Orlando*, Ch. 1
4. James Thomson, *The Seasons* (Winter)
5. John Evelyn, *Diary*, December 1, 1662
6. Marina Warner, *The Skating Party*, Ch. 1
7. ★

E: CHOCOLATE

1. Hilaire Belloc, 'Jim, who ran away from his nurse and was eaten by a lion'
2. Edward Lear, 'By Way of Preface'
3. Graham Greene, *Brighton Rock*, Ch. 2
4. Andrew Marvell, 'Clarendon's Housewarming'
5. Richmal Crompton, *Just William*, 'William's New Year's Day'
6. Samuel Pepys, *Diary*, April 24, 1661
7. ★

FEBRUARY

A: TRANSPORT AND TRAVEL

1. William Brighty Rands, 'The Pedlar's Caravan'
2. Anne Enright, *The Gathering*, Ch. 39
3. T. S. Eliot, 'Skimbleshanks: the Railway Cat'
4. Paul Bowles, *The Spider's House*, last page
5. John Davidson, 'Thirty Bob a Week'
6. G. K. Chesterton, 'The Rolling English Road'
7. *

B: FOG

1. George Gissing, *New Grub Street*, Ch. 8
2. Charles Dickens, *Bleak House*, Ch. 1
3. William Makepeace Thackeray, *Pendennis*, Ch. XXIX
4. Robert Louis Stevenson, *The Strange Case of Dr. Jekyll and Mr. Hyde*, Ch. 4
5. Margery Allingham, *The Tiger in the Smoke*, Ch. 1
6. Jean Rhys, *After Leaving Mr Mackenzie*, Part II, Ch. 1
7. *

C: ALDOUS HUXLEY BOOK TITLES

1. William Shakespeare, *Hamlet*, Act III, i
2. Christopher Marlowe, *Edward II*, Act I, i
3. John Milton, *Samson Agonistes*
4. Alfred, Lord Tennyson, 'Tithonus'
5. William Shakespeare, *The Tempest*, Act V, i
6. William Wordsworth, 'The tables turned. An evening scene on the same subject'
7. *

D: VALENTINES

1. Geoffrey Chaucer, *The Canterbury Tales*, 'Heere taketh the makere of this book his leve' ('Chaucer's Retraction')
2. Edmund Spenser, *The Faerie Queene*, VI, vii

3. John Clare, 'A Valentine', last stanza
4. Robert Herrick, 'To His Valentine, upon S. Valentine's Day'
5. William Shakespeare, *Hamlet*, Act IV, v
6. Thomas Hardy, *Far From the Madding Crowd*, Ch. XIX
7. *

E: SWANS

1. Orlando Gibbons, 'The Silver Swan'
2. W. B. Yeats, 'Leda and the Swan'
3. Laurie Lee, 'Last Days', *Cider with Rosie*
4. Edmund Spenser, 'Prothalamion'
5. John Keats, 'Sonnet to Byron'
6. Aldous Huxley, 'Leda'
7. *

MARCH

A: GHOSTS

1. Horace Walpole, *The Castle of Otranto*
2. Charles Dickens, *A Christmas Carol*, Stave 1
3. Charles Churchill, *The Ghost*, ll. 500–506
4. M. R. James, 'Oh, Whistle, and I'll Come to You, My Lad'
5. Emily Brontë, *Wuthering Heights*, Ch. 3
6. Toni Morrison, *Beloved*, final pages
7. *

B: SNAILS

1. William Shakespeare, 'Venus and Adonis'
2. John Clare, 'Summer Images'
3. Henry James, *The Golden Bowl*, Book II, Ch. 2
4. John Gay, Fable XXIV, 'The Butterfly and the Snail'
5. Lewis Carroll, 'The Lobster Quadrille', *Alice's Adventures in Wonderland*, Ch. X
6. Virginia Woolf, 'The Mark on the Wall'
7. *

C: DRUGS AND MEDICINES

1. Tobias Smollett, *Humphrey Clinker*, Vol. 1, letter to Dr. Lewis
2. W. E. Henley, 'Before'
3. Samuel Taylor Coleridge, letter to John Morgan, May 14, 1814
4. William Burroughs, *The Naked Lunch*, first section
5. William Shakespeare, *Othello*, Act III, iii
6. Thomas De Quincey, 'The Pleasures of Opium', *Confessions of an English Opium-Eater*
7. *

D: WIND

1. Ernest Dowson, 'Non sum qualis eram bonae sub regno Cynarae'
2. William Cowper, *The Task*, Book I, 'The Sofa'
3. Percy Bysshe Shelley, 'Ode to the West Wind'
4. Alfred, Lord Tennyson, *In Memoriam A.H.H.*, XV
5. Angela Carter, *Wise Children*, Ch. 1
6. D. H. Lawrence, 'Song of a Man who has Come Through'
7. *

E: SHIPS AND BOATS

1. Robert Louis Stevenson, *The Wrecker*, Ch. 12
2. Alfred, Lord Tennyson, 'Break, Break, Break'
3. Kenneth Grahame, *The Wind in the Willows*, Ch. 1
4. George Eliot, *The Mill on the Floss*, Book 7, Ch. V
5. Herman Melville, *Moby-Dick*, Ch. 1
6. Derek Walcott, 'A Sea-Chantey'
7. *

APRIL

A: APRIL

1. T. S. Eliot, *The Waste Land*
2. W. H. Davies, 'April's Charms'
3. Ben Jonson, 'An Elegy on the Lady Jane Paulet'
4. Robert Browning, 'Home Thoughts from Abroad'
5. Geoffrey Chaucer, 'Prologue' to *The Canterbury Tales*
6. John Dowland, 'Cleare or cloudie'
7. *

B: HATS AND WIGS

1. Laurence Sterne, *Tristram Shandy*, Vol. III, Ch. VII
2. Edward Lear, 'The Quangle-Wangle's Hat'
3. Oliver Sacks, 'The Man Who Mistook His Wife for a Hat'
4. Zadie Smith, *White Teeth*, Ch. 15
5. Alexander Pope, *The Rape of the Lock*, Canto 1
6. Alice Sebold, *The Lovely Bones*, Ch. 1
7. *

C: RAIN

1. Wilkie Collins, *The Moonstone*, Ch. XIX
2. Henry Thoreau, *Walden*, 'Where I Lived and What I Lived For'
3. Oliver Goldsmith, *The Rising Village*
4. William Golding, *Lord of the Flies*, Ch. 9
5. Christina Rossetti, 'When I Am Dead, My Dearest'
6. James Thomson, *The Seasons*, 'Autumn'
7. *

D: PARIS

1. Jean Rhys, *Good Morning, Midnight*, Part I
2. Charlotte Mew, 'Le sacré cocur'
3. George du Maurier, *Trilby*, Ch. 1
4. Arthur Hugh Clough, *Amours de Voyage*

5. James Joyce, *Ulysses*, Ch. 3
6. Mary Robinson, 'Female Fashions for 1799'
7. *

E: READING

1. Jilly Cooper, *Imogen*, Ch. 1
2. Charlotte Brontë, *Jane Eyre*, Ch. 1
3. Emily Dickinson, Poem 636
4. Jane Austen, *Northanger Abbey*, Ch. 1
5. Mimi Khalvati, 'I'm Reading with the Light On'
6. Alexander Pope, *Essay on Criticism*
7. *

MAY

A: LOVE

1. Charlotte Mew, 'The Farmer's Bride'
2. Sir Philip Sidney, 'My true love hath my heart'
3. Francis Bacon, 'Of Love'
4. Sir Walter Ralegh, 'Walsinghame', last stanza
5. Robert Burton, *The Anatomy of Melancholy*, Part 3
6. Adrian Mitchell, 'Celia, Celia'
7. *

B: KISSES

1. F. Scott Fitzgerald, *The Great Gatsby*, Ch. 6
2. Robert Burns, 'Comin' through the Rye'
3. Hanif Kureishi, *The Buddha of Suburbia*, Ch. 1
4. John Wilmot, Earl of Rochester, 'A Song of a Young Lady to her Ancient Lover'
5. Byron, *Don Juan*, Canto II
6. Leigh Hunt, 'Jenny Kiss'd Me'
7. *

C: MARRIAGE

1. Jane Austen, *Pride and Prejudice*, Ch. 1
2. Evelyn Waugh, *Vile Bodies*, Ch. 11
3. Geoffrey Chaucer, 'General Prologue' to *The Canterbury Tales* (Wife of Bath)
4. Charlotte Brontë, *Jane Eyre*, Ch. XXXVIII
5. Philip Roth, *The Facts*, Ch. 3
6. Ali Smith, *Girl Meets Boy*
7. *

D: SPIDERS

1. M. R. James, 'The Ash Tree'
2. Don Marquis, *Archy and Mehitabel*, vii, 3
3. Iris Murdoch, *Bruno's Dream*, Ch. 14

4. Emily Dickinson, Poem 1275
5. Charles Dickens, *Great Expectations*, Ch.11
6. William Shakespeare, *The Winter's Tale*, II, i
7. *

E: FOUNTAINS

1. D. H. Lawrence, 'Song of a Man Who Has Come Through'
2. P. G. Wodehouse, *The Mating Season*, Ch. 3
3. Kathleen Jamie, 'Fountain'
4. Katherine Philips, 'Friendship'
5. Katherine Mansfield, 'Honeymoon'
6. Aphra Behn, 'The Disappointment'
7. *

JUNE

A: SUNSHINE AND MOONLIGHT

1. Alexander Pope, *The Rape of the Lock*, Canto 1
2. Charles Kingsley, 'The Bad Squire'
3. Samuel Beckett, *Murphy*, Ch. 1
4. John Donne, 'The Sunne Rising'
5. Susan Howe, 'Shelley's Pen Slipped'
6. Sir Philip Sidney, *Astrophil and Stella*, 30
7. *

B: FROGS

1. Emily Dickinson, *Poem* 288
2. John Clare, 'Summer Images'
3. Seamus Heaney, 'Death of a Naturalist'
4. Hilaire Belloc, 'The Frog'
5. Thomas Love Peacock, *Crotchet Castle*, Ch. 6
6. Christina Rossetti, 'A Frog's Fate'
7. *

C: NIGHTINGALES

1. Charlotte Smith, 'To a Nightingale'
2. John Milton, *Paradise Lost*, Book IV
3. Oscar Wilde, 'The Nightingale and the Rose'
4. Mary Robinson, 'Ode to Melancholy'
5. William Shakespeare, *Romeo and Juliet*, Act III, v
6. Edward Thomas, 'Words'
7. *

D: SOLITUDE AND MELANCHOLY

1. Radclyffe Hall, *The Well of Loneliness*, Ch. 8
2. Walter Pater, *The Renaissance*, 'Conclusion'
3. Thomas Hood, 'Ode: Autumn'
4. Ford Madox Ford, *The Good Soldier*, Ch. 1
5. Rachel Cusk, *Outline*, ending

6. Samuel Taylor Coleridge, 'The Rime of the Ancient Mariner'
7. *

E: PARTIES

1. Alfred, Lord Tennyson, *Maud: a Monodrama*
2. William Makepeace Thackeray, *Vanity Fair*, Ch. XXIX
3. Eileen Myles, 'Nice Wishes'
4. Frank O'Hara, 'Alma'
5. Frances Burney, *Evelina*, Letter 11
6. Thomas Moore, 'The Sylph's Ball'
7. *

JULY

A: TIME

1. W. H. Auden, 'Our Bias'
2. Ben Jonson, Kitely, in *Every Man in His Humour*, Act III, ii
3. W. B. Yeats, *The Countess Cathleen*, last lines
4. Archibald MacLeish, 'Ars Poetica'
5. John Keats, 'Sonnet' ('After dark vapors have oppress'd our plains')
6. Andrew Marvell, 'To His Coy Mistress'
7. *

B: OXFORD AND CAMBRIDGE

1. Evelyn Waugh, *Brideshead Revisited*, Ch. 5
2. William Wordsworth, 'Oxford, May 30, 1820'
3. Edward Gibbon, *The Autobiography of Edward Gibbon*
4. Dorothy L. Sayers, *Gaudy Night*, ending
5. Penelope Fitzgerald, *The Gate of Angels*, opening
6. Harold Pinter, *Betrayal*, scene 5
7. *

C: THE SEASIDE

1. D. H. Lawrence, *Sea and Sardinia*, Ch.1
2. Jane Austen, *Persuasion*, Vol. 1, Ch. XII
3. John Fowles, *The French Lieutenant's Woman*, Ch. 2
4. Vladimir Nabokov, *Lolita*, Part 1, 3
5. Carol Ann Duffy, 'Bernadette'
6. W. C. Sellar and R. J. Yeatman, *1066 And All That*, Ch. 51
7. *

D: SUNDAY

1. Marilynne Robinson, *Gilead*, p. 23
2. John Wyndham, *The Day of the Triffids*, Ch. 1
3. George Eliot, *Middlemarch*, Ch. XLVII
4. Percy Bysshe Shelley, 'The Devil's Walk'

5. H. G. Wells, *Kipps*, Ch. 3
6. George Crabbe, Tale XXI: 'The Learned Boy'
7. *

E: HEADACHES

1. Samuel Johnson, *Lives of the Poets*, 'Life of Alexander Pope'
2. Allen Ginsberg, 'A Supermarket in California'
3. Sarah Perry, *After Me Comes the Flood*, Ch. 1, 'Wednesday'
4. Byron, *Don Juan*, Canto II, 179
5. W. S. Gilbert, 'Nightmare', *Iolanthe*
6. Raymond Chandler, *The Long Good-Bye*, Ch. 13
7. *

AUGUST

A: HOLIDAYS

1. W. H. Auden, 'August for the people...'
2. Stanley Middleton, *Holiday*, Ch. 1
3. Anthony Trollope, *The Small House at Allington*, Ch. XLVI
4. Alexander Pope, *The Dunciad*, Book III
5. Beryl Bainbridge, *A Weekend with Claude*, Ch. 2
6. Agatha Christie, *The Mysterious Affair at Styles*, Ch. 1
7. *

B: SWIMMING

1. Deborah Levy, *Swimming Home*, 'Saturday'
2. Rev. Kilvert, *Kilvert's Diary*, Friday 12 June, 1874
3. Margaret Cavendish, Duchess of Newcastle, *Philosophical Fancies*, 'Of the Motions of the Planets'
4. Richard Jefferies, *Bevis*, Ch. 10, 'Savages'
5. Jocelyn Brooke, *Private View*, 'Gerald Brockhurst'
6. Joseph Conrad, 'The Secret Sharer'
7. *

C: KINGFISHERS

1. Sir Thomas Browne, *Pseudodoxia Epidemica*, Book 3, Ch. 8
2. Charles Olson, 'The Kingfishers'
3. Christopher Marlowe, *The Jew of Malta*, Act I, i
4. Stella Gibbons, *Cold Comfort Farm*, Ch. 3
5. Gerard Manley Hopkins, 'As kingfishers catch fire...'
6. T. S. Eliot, 'Burnt Norton'
7. *

D: KNOCKING ON DOORS

1. Lewis Carroll, *Alice's Adventures in Wonderland*, Ch. VI
2. William Shakespeare, *Macbeth*, Act II, iii
3. Raymond Chandler, *The Little Sister*, Ch. 2
4. Andrea Levy, *Small Island*, Ch. 19

5. D. H. Lawrence, 'Song of a Man Who Has Come Through'
6. Jonathan Swift, 'Directions to Servants'
7. ★

E: EVENING

1. William Collins, 'Ode to Evening'
2. Thomas Hardy, *The Return of the Native*, Ch. 1
3. Jane Taylor, 'Evening'
4. Jim Crace, *Harvest*, Ch. 3
5. H.D., 'Evening'
6. Augusta Webster, *Circe*
7. ★

SEPTEMBER

A: TOWN AND COUNTRY

1. William Wordsworth, 'Composed Upon Westminster Bridge, Sept. 3, 1802'
2. William Cowper, *The Task*, Book I, 'The Sofa'
3. Muriel Spark, *The Girls of Slender Means*, Ch. 1
4. Christopher Marlowe, 'The Passionate Sheepheard to his Love'
5. C. Day Lewis, 'Two Songs'
6. John Ruskin, *Sesame and Lilies*, III
7. *

B: POETS

1. Christopher Logue, 'Last Night in Notting Hill'
2. Thomas Hardy, 'Shelley's Skylark'
3. Byron, *Don Juan*, Canto XI, stanza LX
4. Ben Jonson, 'To the Memory of My Beloved the Author, Mr. William Shakespeare'
5. John Wilmot, *Earl of Rochester*, 'Advice to Apollo'
6. John Aubrey, *Brief Lives*, Sir Edmund Waller
7. *

C: REPETITION

1. Lewis Carroll, 'The Hunting of the Snark'
2. Gerard Manley Hopkins, 'God's Grandeur'
3. William Shakespeare, *King Lear*, Act V, iii
4. James Joyce, *Ulysses*
5. John Dowland, 'Say loue if euer thou didst find'
6. A. A. Milne, song from *Winnie-the-Pooh*, Ch. 5
7. *

D: MUSICAL INSTRUMENTS

1. Thomas Hardy, 'Penance'
2. Samuel Taylor Coleridge, 'The Eolian Harp'

3. W. B. Yeats, 'The Fiddler of Dooney'
4. John Bunyan, *The Pilgrim's Progress*, conclusion
5. Rudyard Kipling, 'The Song of the Banjo'
6. Jean Rhys, *Tigers Are Better-Looking*, 'Till September Petronella'
7. *

E: ANGELS

1. Jack Kerouac, *On the Road*, Ch. 12
2. Ben Jonson, *The Sad Shepherd*
3. Evelyn Waugh, *Vile Bodies*, Ch. 6
4. John Milton, *Paradise Regained*, Book I
5. Selima Hill, 'Our Job is to Forget We Are Human'
6. John Donne, 'The Relique'
7. *

OCTOBER

A: CATS

1. Charles Dickens, *Nicholas Nickleby*, Ch. XLIX
2. Thomas Gray, 'Ode: On the Death of a Favourite Cat Drowned in a Tub of Goldfishes'
3. James Boswell, *Life of Samuel Johnson*, 1783
4. Christopher Smart, *Jubilate Agno*
5. James Joyce, *Ulysses*, Ch. 4
6. George Eliot, *Silas Marner*, Ch. 16
7. ⋆

B: CHEESE

1. Anne Sexton, 'The Fury of Cooks'
2. James Joyce, *Ulysses*, Ch. 6
3. R. S. Surtees, *Handley Cross*, Ch. 50
4. R. L. Stevenson, *Treasure Island*, Ch. 15
5. William Shakespeare, *Henry IV Part I*, Act III, i
6. John Lanchester, *The Debt to Pleasure*, 'Another winter menu'
7. ⋆

C: APPLES

1. John Drinkwater, 'Moonlit Apples'
2. John Milton, *Paradise Lost*, Book IX
3. George Borrow, *Lavengro*, Ch. 2
4. Thomas Chatterton, *Ælla* ('Thyrde Minstrelle')
5. W. B. Yeats, 'The Song of Wandering Aengus'
6. Byron, *Cain*, Act II, ii
7. ⋆

D: STARS

1. Amiri Baraka [LeRoi Jones], 'Preface to a Twenty Volume Suicide Note'
2. William Blake, 'Night'

3. George Herbert, 'The Starre'
4. George Meredith, 'Lucifer by Starlight'
5. F. Scott Fitzgerald, *The Great Gatsby*
6. A. E. Housman, *A Shropshire Lad*, LII
7. ★

E: BOREDOM

1. Philip Larkin, 'Dockery and Son'
2. Charles Dickens, *Hard Times*, Book 3, Ch. 2
3. Oscar Wilde, *The Picture of Dorian Gray*, Ch. 9
4. Charles Lamb, 'Poor Relations', *Last Essays of Elia*
5. Byron, *Don Juan*, Canto XIII
6. George Eliot, *Daniel Deronda*, Ch. 13
7. ★

NOVEMBER

A: OWLS

1. Edward Lear, 'The Owl and the Pussy-cat'
2. Alice Oswald, 'Owl Village'
3. Gilbert White, *The Natural History of Selborne*, Letter XV to Barrington
4. John Keats, 'Ode on Melancholy'
5. Thomas Carlyle, *Sartor Resartus*, Ch. III
6. James Thomson, *The Seasons*, 'Winter'
7. ★

B: BONFIRES AND FIREWORKS

1. Thomas Hardy, *The Return of the Native*, Ch. 6
2. Alison Uttley, 'Fires', from *Plowmen's Clocks*
3. Walt Whitman, 'A Song for Occupations', *Leaves of Grass*
4. Sylvia Townsend Warner, 'The Fifth of November', *A Spirit Rises*
5. John Dryden, *Absalom and Achitophel*, II
6. Lewis Carroll, *Through the Looking-Glass*, Ch. 1
7. ★

C: SHOPS AND SHOPPING

1. Patricia Highsmith, *Carol* (or *The Price of Salt*), Ch. 1
2. Saki, 'The Toys of Peace'
3. Christina Rossetti, 'Goblin Market'
4. Daniel Defoe, *Moll Flanders*
5. Louis MacNeice, 'Christmas Shopping', stanza 1
6. Sir Arthur Conan Doyle, 'The Man with the Twisted Lip'
7. ★

D: BATHS

1. Daniel Defoe, *A Tour through England and Wales*, Book II, Letter VI
2. Thomas Hood, 'Stanzas Composed in a Shower-bath'

3. Ford Madox Ford, *The Good Soldier*, Ch. 3
4. Ezra Pound, 'The Bath Tub'
5. Jo Shapcott, 'In the Bath'
6. George & Weedon Grossmith, *The Diary of a Nobody*, April 29, Sunday
7. *

E: WATCHES AND CLOCKS

1. Edgar Allan Poe, 'The Tell-Tale Heart'
2. William Shakespeare, 'Sonnet 19'
3. Charles Dickens, *Master Humphrey's Clock*, Ch. 2
4. William Wordsworth, 'Lucy Gray'
5. Thomas Hardy, *Far From the Madding Crowd*, Ch. 1
6. Henry Wadsworth Longfellow, 'The Old Clock on the Stairs'
7. *

DECEMBER

A: DREAMS

1. Percy Bysshe Shelley, 'Alastor; or the Spirit of Solitude', ll. 149–154
2. W. B. Yeats, 'He Wishes for the Cloths of Heaven'
3. John Donne, 'The Dream'
4. John Keats, letter to Benjamin Bailey, November 22, 1817
5. Edgar Allan Poe, *The Raven*
6. Zora Neale Hurston, *Their Eyes Were Watching God*, Ch. 1
7. *

B: CHRISTMAS

1. Wendy Cope, '19th Christmas Poem'
2. Louisa May Alcott, *Little Women*, Ch. 1
3. Henry Vaughan, 'The True Christmas'
4. Beatrix Potter, 'The Tailor of Gloucester'
5. L. Frank Baum, *The Life and Adventures of Santa Claus*, 'Manhood', Ch. 11
6. James Joyce, *Finnegans Wake*
7. *

C: BELLS

1. Edmund Spenser, 'Epithalamion'
2. Lionel Johnson, 'Bells'
3. Alfred, Lord Tennyson, *In Memoriam A.H.H.*, CVI
4. William Hazlitt, 'On Criticism'
5. Thomas Gray, 'Elegy Written in a Country Church-yard'
6. John Donne, *Devotions Upon Emergent Occasions*, Meditation XVII
7. *

D: COMPASS POINTS

1. John Keats, 'Ode to a Nightingale'
2. Arthur Hugh Clough, 'Say not the struggle...'

3. Aldous Huxley, *Brave New World*, last para
4. Thomas Babington Macaulay, 'Horatius', *Lays of Ancient Rome*
5. Rose Tremain, *The Colour*, Ch. 1
6. Elizabeth Bowen, *To the North*, last pages
7. *

E: DEATH

1. Virginia Woolf, *The Waves*
2. Muriel Spark, *Memento Mori*, Ch. 1
3. Charles Dickens, *The Old Curiosity Shop*, Ch. 71
4. William Shakespeare, *Richard II*, Act III, ii
5. William Wordsworth, 'A slumber did my spirit seal'
6. Joseph Conrad, *Heart of Darkness*
7. *

VALEDICTORY

1. James Boswell, *Life of Samuel Johnson* (Thursday, 6 April 1775)
2. Thom Gunn, 'His Rooms in College'
3. Sir John Harington, 'A Comparison of a Booke, with Cheese'
4. Arnold Bennett, *The Old Wives' Tale*, Ch. IV
5. Robert Browning, 'Soliloquy of the Spanish Cloister'
6. Geoffrey Chaucer, *Troilus and Criseyde*, V, 256
7. Robert Southey, 'Carmen Nuptiale. The Lay of the Laureate', *L'envoy*
8. Robert Louis Stevenson, 'Envoy'
9. Arthur Hugh Clough, *Amours de Voyage*, conclusion
10. Roy Fisher, 'The Making of the Book'

ACKNOWLEDGEMENTS

'Our Bias' from *The Complete Works of W. H. Auden* by W. H. Auden. Text copyright © The W. H. Auden Estate. Published by Princeton University Press and used with permission. • 'August, for the people' from *Another Time* by W. H. Auden. Text copyright © The Estate of W. H. Auden. Published by Faber & Faber (1940) and used with permission. • 'Preface to a Twenty Volume Suicide Note' from *SOS: Poems 1961–2013* (ed. Paul Vangelisti) by Amiri Baraka. Text copyright © Amiri Baraka. Published by Grove Press (2016) and used with permission. • 'Jim, Who Ran Away From His Nurse And Was Eaten By A Lion' from *Cautionary Verses* by Hilaire Belloc. Text copyright © The Estate of Hilaire Belloc. Published by Knopf Doubleday (2013) and used with permission. • 'The Frog' from *The Bad Child's Book of Beasts* by Hilaire Belloc. Text copyright © The Estate of Hilaire Belloc and used with permission. • 'Death in Leamington' from *Collected Poems* by John Betjeman © 1955, 1958, 1962, 1964, 1968, 1970, 1979, 1981, 1982, 2001. Reproduced by permission of John Murray, an imprint of Hodder and Stoughton Limited. • 'Gerald Brockhurst' from *Private View* by Jocelyn Brooke. Text copyright ©Jocelyn Brooke. Published by Robin Clark and used with permission. • '19th Christmas Poem' from *Serious Concerns* by Wendy Cope. Text copyright © Wendy Cope. Published by Faber & Faber (2008) and used with permission. • 'Evening' from *Selected Poems* by Hilda (H. D.) Doolittle. Text copyright © The Estate of Hilda Doolittle. Published by Carcanet Press (1997) and used with permission. • 'Bernadette' from *Collected Poems* by

permission of Georges Borchardt, Inc., on behalf of the Aldous and Laura Huxley Trust. All rights reserved. • 'Fountain' from *Mr and Mrs Scotland Are Dead* by Kathleen Jamie. Text copyright © Kathleen Jamie. Published by Bloodaxe Books (2002) and used with permission. • 'I'm Reading With the Light On' from *Selected Poems* by Mimi Khalvati. Text copyright © Mimi Khalvati. Published by Carcanet Press (2000) and used with permission. • 'Dockery and Son' from *The Whitsun Weddings* by Philip Larkin. Text copyright © The Estate of Philip Larkin. Published by Faber & Faber (2001) and used with permission. • 'The Old Fools' from *High Windows* by Philip Larkin. Text copyright © The Estate of Philip Larkin. Published by Faber & Faber (1979) and used with permission. • 'Two Songs' from The Collected Poems by C. Day Lewis. Text copyright © The Estate of Cecil Day Lewis. Published by Stanford University Press (1996) and used with permission. • 'Last Night in Notting Hill' by Christopher Logue. Text copyright © The Estate of Christopher Logue. Published by The Notting Hill Gate Improvement Group (2002) and used with permission. • 'Ars Poetica' from *Collected Poems 1917–1982* by Archibald MacLeish. Text copyright © The Estate of Archibald Macleish. Published by Houghton Mifflin Harcourt (1985) and used with permission. • 'Christmas Shopping' from Collected Poems by Louis MacNiece. Text copyright © The Estate of Louis MacNiece. Published by Faber & Faber (2016) and used with permission. • Extract from *Winnie the Pooh* by A. A. Milne. Text copyright © The Trustees of the Pooh Properties 1926. Published by Egmont UK Ltd and used with permission. • 'Celia, Celia' from *Greatest Hits* by Adrian Mitchell. Text copyright © Adrian Mitchell. Published by Bloodaxe Books (1991) and used with permission from the Estate of Adrian Mitchell. • Extract taken from 'Nice Wishes' from *Not Me* by Eileen Myles. Text copyright © Eileen Myles. Published by Semiotext(e) (1991) and used with permission. • 'Alma' from *Lunch Poems* by Frank O'Hara. Text copyright © Frank O'Hara.